WILLIAM SHAKESPEARE

THE EXTRAORDINARY LIFE OF THE MOST SUCCESSFUL WRITER OF ALL TIME

BY

ANDREW GURR

PHOTOGRAPHY DIRECTED BY

JULIAN NAPIER

PHOTOGRAPHER

DOMINIC CLEMENCE

HarperCollins*Publishers*

Editor	Susie Elwes
Photographic Director	Julian Napier
Photographer	Dominic Clemence
Associate Producer	Alexandra Ferguson
Casting Directors	Guy Myhill Barry Derbyshire Jon Oram
Costume Designer	Val Metheringham
Set Decorators	Jenny Dyer Elise Napier
Hair and Make-up	Michele Baylis
Photographer's Assistants	Richard Drury Matthew Butler Jonathan Stokes
Production Co-ordinator	Lucy Tylney
Wardrobe Assistants	Becky Loncraine Renata Hall Nikita Rae
Art Department Assistants	Ian Leggett William Russell
Production Assistants	Tiger Bosanquet Ian Dewar Derek Charlton Mike Luscombe Philip Watson
Art Director	Hugh Schermuly
Post Production & Print	Ken Clark
Colour Reproduction	Brian Gregory Associates Ltd St Albans
Created & Produced for HarperCollins Publishers	Hugh Elwes

First published in 1995 by HarperCollins Publishers
77-85 Fulham Palace Road, London W6 8JB

A catalogue record for his book is available from the British Library

ISBN 0 00 470897 0

CONTENTS

Introduction

William Shakespeare is generally accepted as the cleverest user of words in the world. He was born at a particularly fortunate moment in the history of English as a developing language, when print had for the first time made the recording of speech easily available. Over the centuries the English language had developed the speaking skills which set the scene for Shakespeare's arrival on stage. Blank verse had been invented as the best form for spoken poetry in the theatre. The earlier oral tradition of poetry produced rhythm in lines which were easy to remember. Released from rhyming, blank verse provided a flexible basis for rhythmic speech. It was the right moment, too, for the growth of theatre in London. The first professional theatres opened when Shakespeare was in his teens, and by the time he was an adult they were strongly based and ready for him. He was thirty when the first two officially approved companies with their own theatres were established in London, and he was a member of one of them. By the time he died a little over twenty years later his company was patronised by the King, James I, and owned two of its own theatres. He helped to make it rich and pre-eminent. The time was exactly right for him and he was right for his time.

For all his genius as a user of English, Shakespeare took no care to get any of his plays into print. It is lucky for us that a few of his contemporaries, in particular some of his fellow players, published his plays as a memorial to him. In the following centuries thousands of students, editors, and scholars have studied those texts and worked to interpret and explain their subtleties. Set in the light of that huge posthumous industry, the very ordinariness of Shakespeare's upbringing, his plain home and much of his working life, including the twenty or so years he spent in London working on his plays and acting in them, makes both their creation and their survival almost unbelievable, and an incredible piece of good fortune.

But too often this piece of luck has been converted into an educational goal, to be achieved by analysing every word rather than using the text as script for living theatre. That is part of the price Shakespeare's work now has to pay for the praise that has been rightly heaped on it. This book is an attempt to return Shakespeare to some of the realities of his own time. It presents a reasonably faithful replication in pictures of his life and his work and

first appearance at the Globe playhouse its hero Hamlet fixed himself in people's imaginations. Writers immediately started using his character in their own plays. The succeeding centuries have done the same, in different forms and in many different languages. Russian literature up to the revolution in 1917 is full of Hamlets. All this attention over the centuries makes it difficult to get back to the original conditions of the year 1600 or 1601 when it first appeared.

the conditions of his time as he experienced them. It records the best of what we know about his life and his times, about his fellow-actors and the theatres they worked in, and about the plays he wrote for them.

His plays were originally composed in order to function merely as scripts for acting on stage. That makes the creation of such a set of intricate verbal structures, now part of the fabric of human thought, seem the more improbable when we see the conditions which produced them. It makes us think of Shakespeare's plays as his friend Ben Jonson described them, "not of an age, but for all time". But they were very much of his age and time.

Plays like *Hamlet* have become part of our thinking and our language. A book or an article is published about one or another aspect of *Hamlet* every day on average, and hundreds of stage productions are performed in different languages every year. From the first weeks of its

Hamlet as a story was a radical concept in its own time. It showed things that people had been feeling but, under the pressures of conventional thinking, had no way until then of bringing to life. In a strongly Christian society, human communities were assumed to be essentially good. Communal life was the norm. Outsiders were rebels, outlaws, social failures. Heroes were all leaders, doers of good for the sake of an inherently good society. *Hamlet* made its hero an outcast who first appears sulking on stage dressed for a funeral when everyone else is dressed for a wedding, his own mother's. He hates his mother and his new stepfather, and what he thinks is his mother's sexual casualness makes him disenchanted with womankind generally. In the standard view of his time such feelings would make him evil, a dangerous misanthrope. Shakespeare made him the first heroic outcast, the first rebel who proves to be morally and psychologically superior to the society in which he lives. In these days, when we have come to believe automatically in progress, and that change is usually for the better, when we expect to make heroes of the individualist, it is not easy to see how radical *Hamlet* was. *Hamlet's* creation triggered the change to the modern view that the individual is better than society.

That is a large claim to make for one play written for money by a player in an acting company at a time when acting was regarded as only one step above beggary. But Shakespeare's quality does not depend on such claims. The range of his verbal skills, his wit and comic inventiveness, the complexity and intensity of his tragic constructs, his sensitivity to human weakness shown in a multitude of characters and relationships, had an instant appeal which has stood the test of time. Just a very few examples from the same play will show a little of this range.

It was not new to have plays and other forms of literature in which the hero soliloquises, talking to himself about his problems. In Greek and Roman plays, which Shakespeare often used as a source, such soliloquies were framed in arguments which reached a conclusion. Hamlet's "To be or not to be" speech was striking in its expression of self-doubt, its lack of any resolution. This was an all too human voice, laden with anguished indecision. It struck an immediate chord in the minds of the first audiences, and has done so ever since. Verbal inventiveness is evident in such famous scenes as the gravedigger's dialogue. In the game of verbal fencing between Hamlet and the gravedigger we forget that Hamlet is joking with the man digging a grave for his beloved Ophelia, who he does not yet know has died. Comedy and tragedy mingle painfully in this new kind of invention.

There is a similar discomfort when Hamlet makes a painful pun after his first meeting with his father's ghost and learns about the murder. He clutches his head with the pain of his new knowledge, and swears that he will remember the ghost "While memory holds a seat / In this distracted globe". We can immediately see the pun he makes on the "distracted" (which also means mad) audience at the Globe playhouse. It is an unfolding pun which alludes also to Hamlet contrasting himself with Hercules, the figure who was depicted on the Globe's flag. The Globe playhouse took its name from the story of Hercules holding the celestial globe on his shoulders

while its designated holder, Atlas, fetched the apples of the Hesperides for him. Hamlet's head on his shoulders is a burden like Hercules's load, the globe. Hamlet, the thinking man and student, contrasts himself in his mad and distracted state with Hercules, the classical man of action. The pun is both a joke against the first theatre audiences at the Globe and Hamlet's expression of his own agony and the threat of madness.

Shakespeare holds a wealth of riches for everyone. The stories themselves, most of them taken from published histories or tales around in Shakespeare's time, and dramatised with incredible ingenuity and potency; the language, voiced most famously in the heroics of *Henry V* and his rousing speech to his soldiers before Agincourt, or Mercutio's set-piece speech about Queen Mab; the scenes of high comedy, from Kate in *The Taming of the Shrew* to Malvolio in *Twelfth Night*; and above all the small touches which make characters and moments human and recognisable, are infinitely various. They will shine in different lights for different people. But the best light is that of their own time, the context which illuminates Shakespeare's texts. The text is not just a trampoline for the sophisticated wordgames it contains, and which we have learned to bounce on in the last four centuries. We should not let them conceal the multiplicity of other qualities that he originally conceived for the plays.

CHAPTER ONE

STRATFORD

IN THE SIXTEENTH CENTURY Stratford was a small town on the banks of the river Avon in Warwickshire, a fertile farming region. As the largest market for the local farmers it was peopled by corn chandlers, millers, wool merchants and the traders, dealers, craftsmen and artisans who manufactured the bread, ale, candles, feather beds and all the other chattels of provincial life.

Its Tudor bridge across the Avon still stands and now as then is used by the town's heavy traffic. It was built at the end of the fifteenth century by Sir Hugh Clopton, a local man who made his fortune in London as a mercer or cloth seller. He became Lord Mayor of London in 1491. The permanence of the crossing at this point on the Avon allowed Stratford to flourish as a major trade route. Travellers from London still have to cross the Clopton bridge to reach Stratford town.

The church, Holy Trinity, stands by the river in the oldest part of town. At about the time of Shakespeare's baptism there, on 26 April 1564, the wall and ceiling paintings and elaborate Catholic decorations were painted over and removed. The Reformation, the new religious order brought in by Henry VIII when he fell out with the Pope in 1534, focused on the pulpit to carry its message rather than the high altar. Every Sunday the whole town met here to worship, to listen, to see and to be seen. As well as a custom it was also an obligation which kept the whole community together and protected.

Shakespeare was a common name in Warwickshire in the sixteenth century and there were two families of the name living at the time in Stratford. William Shakespeare's father, John, was an important citizen whose craft was leatherwork and whittawering, working in white leather to make gloves, aprons and purses. He came from a yeoman family. Yeomen rented the greater part of the land they farmed as tenants. Their lives depended on the weather and the harvest. John Shakespeare moved into Stratford town to become a citizen, a freeman earning his living from a town trade. His business flourished and his importance as a leading citizen grew rapidly.

In 1557 he married Mary Arden, one of the daughters of an old landowning and farming family from near Stratford. The youngest of her parents' eight or more daughters, she was evidently the family favourite, and inherited most of her father's property at his death in 1556. She married John Shakespeare not long after her father died.

__William Shakespeare's__ parents both grew up on farms close to Stratford. Like most English towns it revolved around country life.

Her first daughter was born in 1558, and another daughter was born in 1562.

__Shepherds__, blacksmiths and milk maids were an important part of the rural community.

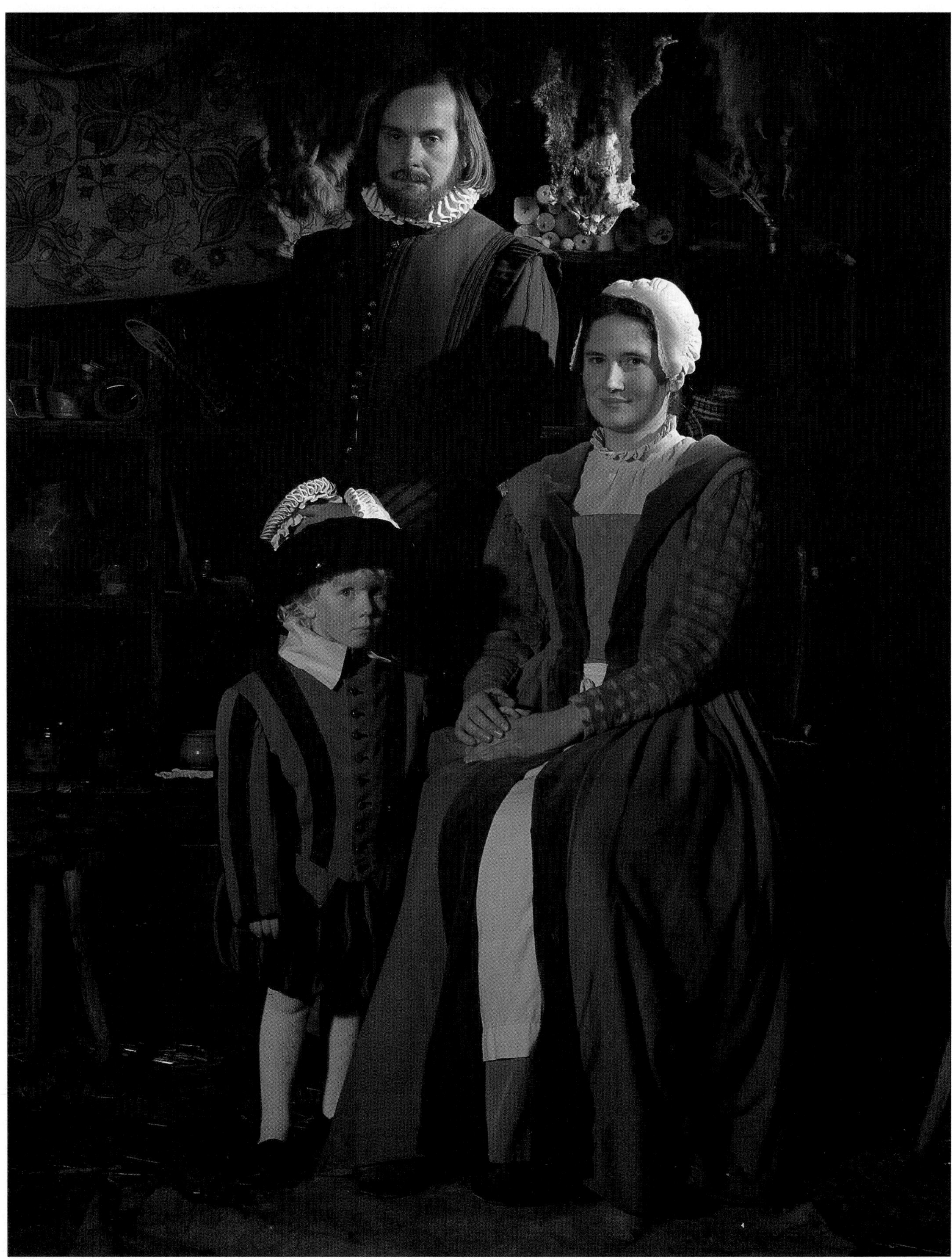

John and Mary Shakespeare *with their eldest child William.*

Bubonic Plague

The bubonic plague first appeared in Europe in 1348 and continued as a major hazard to life in England until the end of the seventeenth century. One epidemic in 1625 killed one-fifth of the whole population of England. The plague was transmitted by fleas which lived on the black rat, but could survive on humans. The plague bacillus usually remained dormant in colder weather, but almost every summer as the days grew warmer there would be an epidemic somewhere in England. Rats were everywhere, in town and country, and the plague spread rapidly. In the country nothing could be done to protect the farming communities against it. In the larger towns strict laws were enforced, prohibiting assemblies of people anywhere except at church. It was not until late in the seventeenth century, when the black rat's ecological niche was taken over by a brown rat ,which did not carry the plague flea, that the epidemics of bubonic plague ceased in England. Shakespeare was lucky to escape a severe outbreak of the plague in Stratford in his birth-year, 1564. His family was among the fifty per cent or less of families in the area which did not lose one or more members to the plague.

A bedroom scene *shows the passage of the plague. There are two patients in one bed, a doctor examines a flask of urine. There was however no cure. On the floor an open coffin waits to be filled by the body laid out near by.*

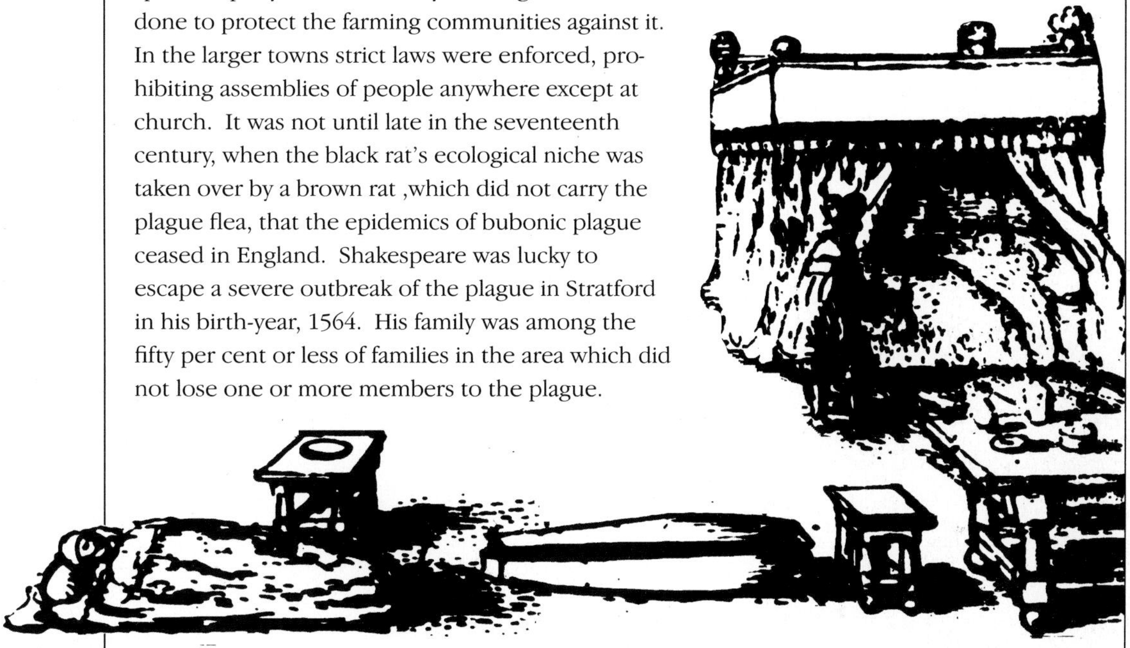

William was her third child and the first to survive more than a few months. Five more children followed. Three boys, Gilbert, Richard, and Edmund, and a sister, Joan, survived childhood. The youngest, Edmund, was baptised on 3rd May 1580.

The high infant mortality rate was not the only hazard that small children had to run before reaching maturity. Epidemics of plague, fires and other natural disasters were risks for every age. It was generally a peaceful time and England was tightly governed. Everyone was enrolled in his or her parish and travellers were regarded with suspicion. There were laws against 'sturdy beggars', the able-bodied trying to make a living on the road by begging. In rural and wooded areas such as Warwickshire fire was always a hazard, and the arrival of licensed travellers from the highway also meant the plague was a regular visitor.

John Shakespeare, glover and whittawer, is described in the town records by his occupation, a medieval custom from the time when the guilds of craftsmen were more important. But like all small businessmen of his time he had many other money-making ventures. Besides leather goods, he also dealt in wool, and seems to have been a fairly general trader in farm products. From his wife's inheritance he owned land in Wilmcote, and acquired more, some to use and some to rent out. His success as a town trader is reflected in his rapid rise in rank in the town council, the local governing system.

The first house John Shakespeare bought was in Henley Street near the market place. He added the neighbouring house and garden in 1557 before his marriage and built a link-block to make them into one. Tudor houses were normally made out of timber frames set on brick foundations. The walls were simply filled in with woven sticks covered with mud and dung or more expensive oak staves and plaster. It was a very simple matter to add on new timber frames and extensions.

It was normal for craftsmen and traders to use a part of their house as a workroom or storeroom, another part as their shop and living quarters, and find a space for apprentices, boys who were learning the craft under the guild system which survived from medieval times.

John Shakespeare became one of the principal citizens of Stratford. From about 1560 he was one of the fourteen burgesses who made up the town council. The council met each morning at 9 o'clock to deal with the town's affairs. They heard petitions and adjudicated complaints between citizens. They were responsible for the state of the water supply, streets and town market. Regular checks were kept on fair trading especially to ensure that weights and measures were accurate and that the beer and ale sold was wholesome. Ale-taster was one of the first positions held by John Shakespeare. Ale, unlike beer, was not flavoured with hops, although both were produced by fermenting barley. It was a job for a discreet and sober man and important in a town famous for its breweries. As a young trader, John Shakespeare rose rapidly through the system from chamberlain to alderman to the highest rank of all as bailiff. When he became an alderman he was entitled to wear a fur trimmed black gown and an alderman's thumb ring on all public occasions. Rank was defined by ceremony as well as costume and for his year of office as bailiff he was escorted to the guild hall by uniformed sergeants. He was expected to sit in front at church, and at the guild chapel. He had the duty of setting the weekly price of corn and thereby bread and ale. He could also apply to the College of Heralds in London, to be granted a coat of arms, making him a gentleman, which of course he did. He did not however receive this next step up in social rank immediately.

All the evidence suggests, however, that by about 1576 John Shakespeare had fallen on hard times. On several occasions he was unable to pay his debts. He stopped attending council meetings. His alderman's seat

__William__ and his brother Gilbert in their father's shop.

__Glove making__ was only one side of John Shakespeare's profession. The fine, soft, white leather needed to make gloves, purses and aprons was produced by whittawering. Tawering was the medieval name for producing leather from animal skins. Whittawering meant simply treating certain types of skins to produce stretchy white leather. Goat, known as kid, and pig skins were soaked in a salt solution. Egg yolk and flour formed part of the dressing. It was a smelly, messy process which was kept as far as possible outside in the open air.

was left open for him and his subscription towards equipping soldiers was reduced, though it was still not paid. He was not required to pay four pennies weekly towards poor relief, nor was he fined for non-attendance at the council. Indeed, no replacement as an alderman was made until 1586 although he last attended a council meeting in 1582. His fellow councillors must have gone on hoping he would return.

At home in the face of growing debts John began to raise money through mortgages and land sales. The Shakespeares eventually lost all the property that both Mary and John had inherited because they failed to keep up mortgage payments and were forced to sell for low sums. They received £4 for their share in two cottages and 100 acres at Snitterfield in 1579. John stood bail of £10 for his brother Henry and £10 for a Stratford tinker, both of which sums he lost. To protect and secure his property he continued to sue and be sued as actively as he had chased money through the courts before. The law courts were regularly used by all buinessmen at the time.

If the records do not reveal John Shakespeare's problems in every detail they do show that he was not alone with his financial troubles. It was noted by government officials that there was great economic hardship in Warwickshire and the surrounding counties which worsened towards the end of the century. By 1601 the poor of Stratford numbered 700 of all ages, which was about half the population of the town. Bad harvests in the 1590s meant the poor in the countryside starved and died. The town of Stratford was twice devastated by fires in September 1594 and 1595 which destroyed about one hundred and twenty eight houses and eighty other buildings. Houses were burned in Henley Street while the Shakepeares continue to live in their house there.

The church and the Guild chapel also survived the fires. Since the Act of Unity passed by Queen Elizabeth's first parliament in 1559 all churches had been ordered to follow the same path using the same specified books, the Book of Commmon Prayer, the English Bible, the new Kalendar, the Psalter, two books of Homilies and a paraphrase of Erasmus in English.

The Act successfully established an exclusively Protestant form of worship throughout England and Wales. It concluded Henry VIII's quarrels with the Pope

The Spanish Armada

The great Spanish Armada was a fleet of 130 ships launched by Philip II of Spain against England in May 1588. It carried an entire army of invasion and administrators to take over England. There were several great battles fought in the English channel. Once the Armada was blown out of the channel the immediate threat of invasion passed. The English navy was lucky to be able to leave it to the wind and storms to destroy most of the Spanish ships trying to return home.

The Spanish Armada fought the last battle in a long running war between English pirates successfully raiding Spanish treasure ships carrying gold from the Americas home to Spain. Piracy was a very profitable part of English naval tactics. The light, and fast, English frigates had already proved superior to the heavy Spanish galleons in manoeuvering at sea. This previously undeclared war included the circumnagivation of the world by Sir Francis Drake in 1577 as part of English naval policy to attack Spanish shipping.

***The great Spanish invasion fleet**, launched by Philip II, was defeated overwhelmingly by bad weather, indecision, misfortune and English naval tactics. The Armadas raised later by Philip never carried the same threat of invasion to England as the great Armada of 1588.*

Stratford *had been granted the right to govern its own affairs as a corporation. The head of the town council was the bailiff appointed by the fourteen aldermen. The aldermen also chose fourteen burgesses to assist them in their duties. These duties ranged from petitioning the Crown for financial help to keeping the peace between neighbours. Their daily concern was to run the town market. To ensure fair trading they regularly checked weights and quality of the town's traders.*

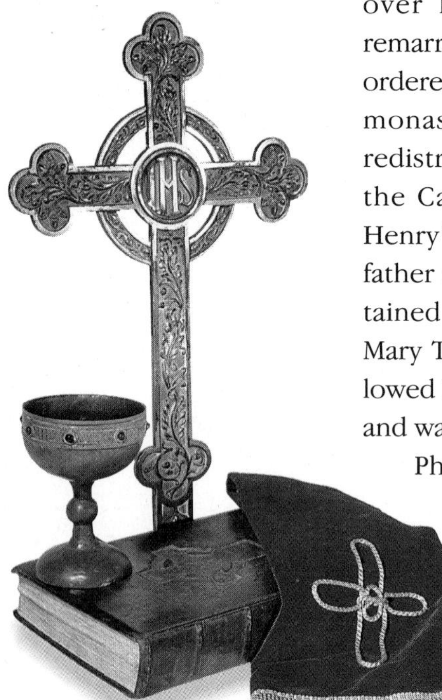

Mary Tudor's persecution *of Protestants during her brief reign earned her the title of "Bloody Mary". Her half-sister Elizabeth I continued the persecutions but her victims were Catholics. The Privy Council authorised torture to obtain information. The cruelty of Norton, the Queen's "rack-master", incited public revulsion so Elizabeth licensed her most effective agent Topcliffe to torture "in private". The rack caused such dislocation and damage that Topcliffe chose to hang men, by their hands, so their feet could not touch the ground. It was a fortunate man who was sentenced to be hanged by the neck until dead. Otherwise he could suffer quartering, and disembowelment while still just alive following hanging.*

over his divorce and remarriage. Henry VIII had ordered the dissolution of the monasteries and the sale and redistribution of lands owned by the Catholic Church. Edward VI, Henry's only son, who succeeded his father as king for a brief six years maintained the Protestant Church in England. Mary Tudor, Henry VIII's eldest daughter, followed her young stepbrother as Queen in 1553 and was a devout Catholic.

Philip II of Spain, an equally fervent Catholic, married Mary Tudor in 1554 so she became Queen of England and Spain. She and Philip had no children of their own. At her death in 1558, her stepsister Elizabeth, also a daughter of King Henry VIII, became Queen of England. Elizabeth I was not recognized as the legitimate heir to the English throne by the Pope, as head of the Catholic Church. The Pope had refused to grant a divorce to her father Henry VIII from his first wife, Catherine of Aragon, who was Mary Tudor's mother. As Elizabeth was born before Catherine died the Catholic Church ruled that neither Henry VIII's marriage to her mother Anne Boleyn nor her own birth could be regarded as legitimate and therefore she was not the rightful successor to the English throne.

The rich and powerful Catholic rulers in Europe, followed the Pope's ruling and supported their own Catholic candidate, Mary Queen of Scots, as the rightful heir to the English throne. Mary was the only daughter of Henry VIII's sister Margaret. She succeeded her father, James V, as Queen of Scotland in 1542. Mary was forced to flee from Scotland because of her lack of judgement and good government. She left her son, James VI, behind. She sought shelter in England with her cousin Elizabeth, who was threatened by her presence, as a Catholic rallying point for revolt from within England. To be a Catholic in Queen Elizabeth's England was to be thought an enemy of the Queen.

In 1591 the hierarchy of the Protestant Church was newly inspired by its leader, the Archbishop of Canterbury, to examine its spiritual appearance. Every parish in the land had to check on recusants, puritans and particularly Catholics, within their boundaries. Recusants were identified as those who failed to attend church once a month. The churchwardens in Stratford published a list

of them in March 1591 which included John Shakespeare. Whether his absence was for religious reasons or more practical concerns is open to question. A year later a second parish report said that all the nine men named in the previous report were avoiding church in order to escape being prosecuted for repayment of debts. Those identified as Catholics who had agreed to conform to the Protestant faith were reported with satisfaction.

A great deal of effort has been spent trying to establish John Shakespeare's religious beliefs. Documents were discovered in the eighteenth century hidden in his Henley Street house, which are consistent with secret Catholic worship. Stratford was home to extreme puritans like Robert Perrott, a brewer, and Catholics like the Cawdrey family, tradesmen, who also held high office in Stratford, no doubt with some difficulty, but openly.

The King's New School in Stratford is still used as part of the Stratford Grammar School. In the 1560s the town council appointed and paid the schoolmaster to educate the sons of the town. Families who could afford to educate girls considered needlework, singing and playing music on the lute or an early keyboard instrument called the virginals as proper schooling, although girls in some towns were admitted to the first stage of school.

It is difficult to know how many people in the Tudor population at large could read and write. Scholars have compared the proportions of people who signed documents with their names against those who signed with a cross, but that ignores the way many used a cross as a holy sign, like a formal oath, when they signed a paper. John Shakespeare signed with either a cross or a pair of compasses, a measuring tool of his glove-making trade. Usually on town business clerks and scriveners prepared documents for signature, and the councillors, many of whom we know from other evidence could write long letters for themselves, would sign with their mark rather than their name. The practice varied widely. One of Shakespeare's daughters, Susanna, signed her papers with her full name, but her sister, Judith, signed with a cross. Women could often read, though they were not usually taught to write as well. Queen Elizabeth was exceptional in speaking and writing fluent Latin as well as English. She was more literate than some of her male councillors. Her example stimulated a marked increase in the number of women poets and writers.

A boy's education began at the age of four or five, not in the grammar school proper but in a "petty" school. An "usher" or teaching assistant had the "tedious task" of teaching the alphabet from a "horn book". The children progressed to reading and writing the abc and the catechism and in some schools simple arithmetic was taught. In two years, with study of the psalms and devotional matter, the boys were ready for the Grammar School.

There were two schoolmasters in charge of the King's New School during William Shakespeare's youth. Simon Hunt taught from 1571 until 1575. Later, he left to attend the university in France favoured by English Catholics, and in Rome he became a Jesuit. His successor was

***A horn book** was made from a page of paper framed on wood and protected by a transparent piece of horn. The alphabet was written in small letters and capitals and often there was room to include the Lord's Prayer. Horn books were used by the youngest children learning to read and write.*

***In William Shakespeare's words** "Creeping like snail unwilling to school". The school day began at dawn, about 6 o'clock, and finished at 5 o'clock, with breaks for breakfast and dinner. There were few holidays. In the school hierarchy the school master in Stratford was a figure of authority.*

Adult strength *is needed to shoot a long bow. Boys practise with small horn bows. They take aim but raise their bows to shoot, so the curved trajectory of the arrow will allow it to hit the target.*

Archery

Boys were also expected to take physical exercise as they grew, to strengthen themselves for adult life. Roger Ascham, a distinguished writer about education, who taught Queen Elizabeth in her youth, published a dialogue in 1545, subtitled "The schole of shootinge". It advocated archery as the best possible sport for the youth of England, and the best accompaniment to study. "In Studie every part of the body is idle, which thing causeth gross and cold humours to gather together and vex scholars very much...Running, leaping and quoiting be too vile for scholars...walking alone into the fields hath no token of courage in it. Therefore if a man would have a pastime wholesome and equal to every part of the body, pleasant and full of courage for the mind, not vile and unhonest...let him seek chiefly of all other things for shooting". Such encouragement, combined with a nostalgia for the English long bow, which had secured Henry V's victory against the French at Agincourt a century before, made archery a very popular sport.

***Public butts** were set up for practice in many towns and villages. Place names often contain the word butts, such as Newington Butts on London's south bank.*

Thomas Jenkins, a graduate from Oxford, who served from 1575 to 1579. The school records giving the names of the pupils have not survived, but William must have been one of them. Only William Smith, a fellow pupil has been traced as continuing his studies at Oxford University.

Grammar school education meant learning Latin, the language used by scholars, lawyers and doctors and for writing official documents. The boys started reading the principles of Latin grammar in English. They mastered the language by memorising Latin texts and reciting them out loud. Usually housed in one room, the school pupils worked their way from lower to upper school.

They also worked progressively through classical Latin literature and more recent works in Latin by Erasmus and Mantuanus. In prose they started with Cato, learning style from Quintilian and later Cicero. They studied and recited the poetry and plays of Palingenius, Terence and, in the upper school, the poems of Ovid. One set task was to translate a Latin bible into English. They wrote compositions and poems in Latin. They may have had to memorize the Latin vocabulary of Withal's *Short Dictionary*. Recitation of poetry led to composition and the performance of speeches. They studied prose style as rhetoric. Public speaking, known as oratory, speaking in Latin to an audience, was highly valued. History was learnt from Caesar among others. In the upper school Greek construction from the New Testament was undertaken.

Although Latin was declining in its use as an "official" language, it was still recognised as a sign of a well-educated man. The universities provided professional education in divinity, law and medicine, but did not at that time go any further in the study of literature.

William was about fourteen when his father began to have his money troubles. John may have found the few pennies for the schoolmaster each week too expensive. He may have thought his son was already well schooled. He would certainly not have been able to afford to send him to university.

The sons of craftsmen usually began to work in the family business under the guild system of training or apprenticeship. Around the age of fourteen a boy would go to live with a master and work in his workshop learning

Sonnet 145

Those lips that love's own hand did make
Breathed forth the sound that said 'I hate'
To me that languished for her sake;
But when she saw my woeful state,
Straight in her heart did mercy come,
Chiding that tongue that ever sweet
Was used in giving gentle doom,
And taught it thus anew to greet:
'I hate' she altered with an end
That followed it as gentle day
Doth follow night who, like a fiend,
From heaven to hell is flown away,
'I hate' from hate away she threw,
And saved my life, saying 'not you'.

***Young lovers** can escape the law and social conventions, but not the consequences of their actions when Anne Hathaway found herself pregnant .*

his craft for around seven years. Within this time he became a skilled craftsman and therefore qualified to work for a wage and to seek a new employer if his master had no room or insufficient income to employ him in his own workshop. At the end of his apprenticeship he became a member of the craft guild.

William Shakespeare married when he was eighteen. Apprentices, dependent on living with their masters, and undergraduates at the universities and lawcourts, were not permitted to marry. Even if he was working in his father's craft shop, he evidently did not have the status of an apprentice. His wife, Anne Hathaway, was quite a good catch for the son of a citizen with growing debts, though she was several years older than William. The house now known as Anne Hathaway's cottage in Shottery to the south of Stratford was then called Hewlands Farm. It was a twelve-roomed house, a much more substantial residence than a cottage. Her father, Richard Hathaway, was a successful yeoman farmer. Anne was the eldest of his three daughters and about twenty five when her father died, leaving her ten marks to be paid on her wedding day. She married William a year later.

It does seem to have been a romantic match, rather than one arranged by the parents, as commonly happened in Tudor England. William preserved a sonnet written to Anne amongst his private papers, his collection of 154 sonnets. The sonnet, Number 145, is unique in being written in different metre to the others. Its punch-line is a controlled pun on Anne's surname, Hathaway. A pun is a play on words and here William used the English word "hate", meaning to dislike intensely, to play on Anne's family name Hathaway in a clever word game.

What the exact Stratford pronunciation of "Hathaway" was we can only guess, but it evidently satisfied the eighteen-year-old William. That this strange and immature sonnet was preserved for twenty seven years in Shakespeare's papers before it slipped into print along with the other collected Sonnets is a remarkable testimony to the author's secret possessiveness about his early work. It is thought to be the only example of his early writings and we have to assume that he destroyed or kept hidden everything else he wrote in his youth.

William may have wooed Anne with poetry, but he also made her pregnant. They married in 1582, and their first daughter was born five months later. The general expectation about young men was that, whether they were humble apprentices or ambitious students, they could not think of marriage until they had completed their studies and become wage earners. Apprenticeships, and scholarly studies, whether traditional rhetoric at Oxford and Cambridge or law at the Inns of Court, did not end until a man was at least twenty one. The usual age for a man to marry was roughly between twenty four and twenty eight. To marry at eighteen was a rare privilege, one usually confined to the sons of the very rich.

Certainly Anne was older than William, and was at about the standard age for marriage. The peculiarity of her marriage to William lay in his youth. There are some signs of haste in the preparation of the wedding documents. It was not the usual time of year to get married and Anne's pregnancy may have been the deciding factor.

The key issues would have been whether William had the maturity and skill to support a family. The marriage was between the children of old friends, and Anne's mother and William's parents may have thought William capable. As it turned out, they were right.

CHAPTER TWO

THE LOST YEARS

William Shakespeare must have started married life in Henley Street, living in his parents' house and working in the shop. How long this lasted we do not know. Almost nothing is known about what he did in the next few years. His marriage prevented him from studying at university. It is most likely that he worked for his father for some years, presumably in a serious attempt to pull his fortunes back from the decline of the last ten years.

If that was William's initial purpose, clearly he failed to achieve it. There is nothing in the records to say why John Shakespeare's various businesses: the whittawer shop-work, the wool merchandising, and his smaller enterprises, were not providing enough income for the three generations of Shakespeares occupying the house in Henley Street. The only evidence in the records is the recurrent sale of the inherited lands and other properties through the 1580s. William's contribution to his father's business made no difference to that. Any cash realised went into the household coffers, and provided food and other comforts for the dozen or more Shakespeares and their helpers at the house. Government officials reported economic hardship throughout the north midlands. Within the next twenty years, by 1601, the poor in Stratford numbered 700, nearly half the population.

William must have known he had skill in writing for which, in a small market town like Stratford, there was no use, let alone profit. The family's financial troubles may have made him restless, and given him good reason to look further afield to see if he could improve the family fortunes elsewhere. But it was not easy to travel. The whole of England was divided into parishes, and each parish had the responsibility of looking after its own poor. To travel freely you needed not only money but a licence. Laws existed to imprison healthy folk who took to the road without good reason or evidence that they had the sort of skills that could make a traveller self-sufficient. There was a strong statute declaring that any travellers who looked like "beggars and sturdy vagabonds" should be arrested in whatever parish they passed through. However, many youths from the poorer country areas slipped off to London, where the pot of gold that Dick Whittington found was thought to be available to all.

Some Stratfordians did establish themselves successfully in London, but they normally did so from a secure basis as traders with goods to sell. Sir Hugh Clopton was a Stratford model of this kind, and others, including in later years Shakespeare's brother Gilbert, followed his path to London. One of Shakespeare's contemporaries, Richard Field, got to London, learned a trade as a printer, and eventually secured a permanent place for himself in the business by marrying his master's widow. But mostly such hopefuls had resources behind them greater than those of the Shakespeare family in the 1580s. They were also unmarried.

William and Anne's first child Susanna was born in May 1583. Twins followed in February 1585, named Judith and Hamnet after family friends. The only boy, Hamnet, died in 1596 aged eleven. It was an unusually small family for the time, when the death rate among young children was so high. Large families ensured that enough children would survive into adulthood to support and provide for their parents in old age.

Anne stayed in Stratford all her life, while William travelled and settled to work in London. He did not return to live with his family properly until 1609, after more than twenty years away. In his time away from Stratford as a professional actor and writer, the only time he had to visit

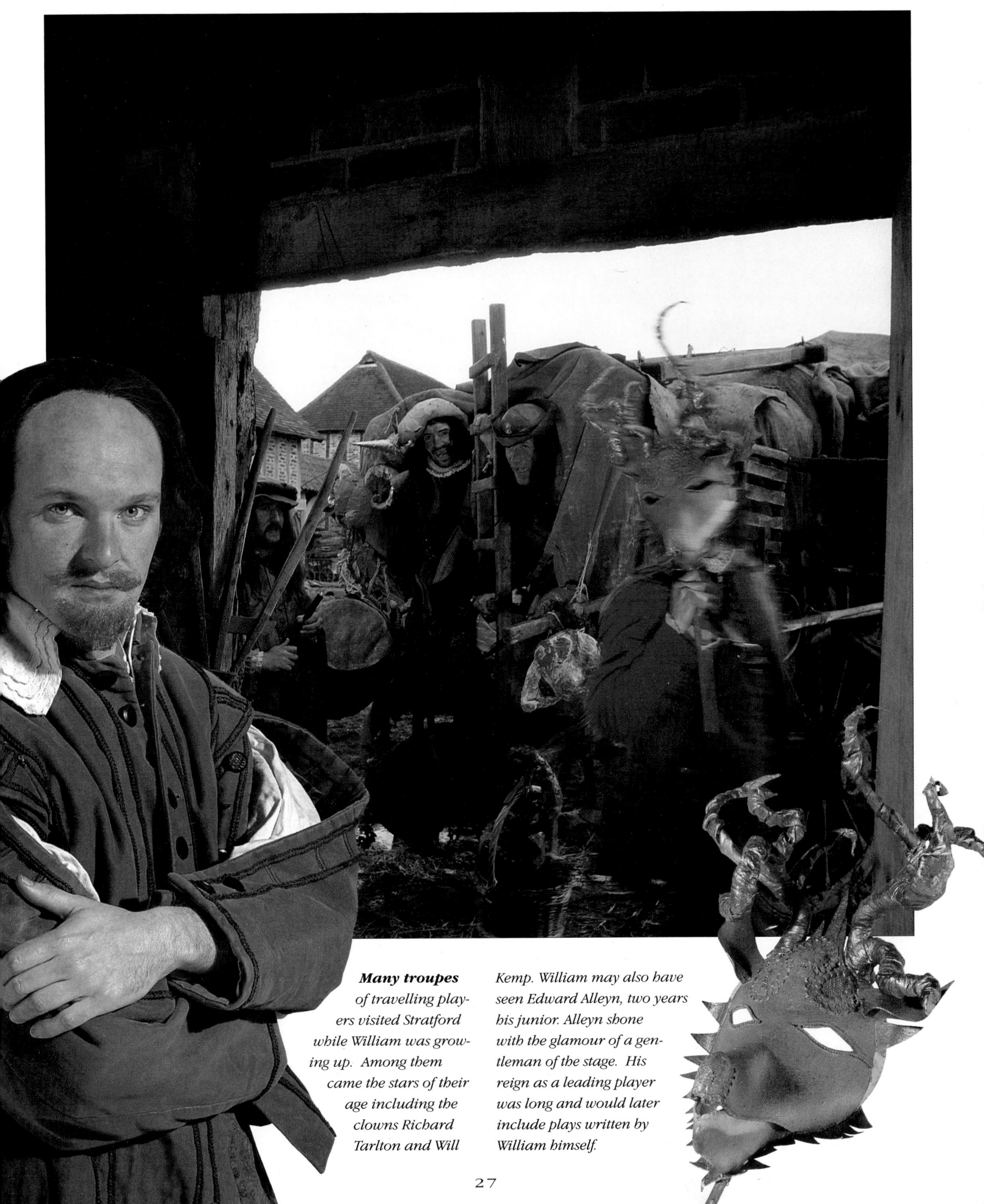

Many troupes *of travelling players visited Stratford while William was growing up. Among them came the stars of their age including the clowns Richard Tarlton and Will Kemp. William may also have seen Edward Alleyn, two years his junior. Alleyn shone with the glamour of a gentleman of the stage. His reign as a leading player was long and would later include plays written by William himself.*

William's first child *Susanna was christened on 26th May, 1583. William, Anne and the baby would have crowded into John and Mary Shakespeare's house in Henley Street. The house bulged with three family generations. William's mother may have welcomed the extra help from Anne. William's only surviving sister Joan was aged thirteen, his youngest brother Edmund was three years old.*

his family each year were the forty days of Lent. Then all forms of entertainment were officially banned, although the London theatres would remain open for as long as possible into the start of the churches' observance of the forty days of the Easter cycle.

Stratford was four days ride from London. The theatre company William joined in London in 1594 regularly toured country towns and houses when the London theatres closed because of epidemics of the plague. Even so, there are no records of any company visiting Stratford in central Warwickshire while William was a member. Indeed after his retirement to Stratford the town council made it unlawful for players to perform.

Anne was a loyal and strong woman, who reaped at least some profit from her husband's absence when, in 1597, he bought her the second biggest house in town, New Place. Anne and the children shared John and Mary Shakespeare's house in Henley Street previously. The upturn in William's fortunes came from his earnings as a player, writer and shareholder in the London theatre company. The rewards of his talent and energy were all invested back in Stratford in houses, land and tithes.

Anne was to outlive her husband by seven years. Her eldest daughter Susanna was married happily to an eminent local doctor, John Hall, and had a daughter. Judith, younger daughter and surviving twin, married a less reputable Stratford wine merchant, Thomas Quiney, just before her father's death. Their first son, Shakespeare Quiney, died in infancy. Two other sons died within weeks of each other as young men and the whole family line died out in the seventeenth century.

The entertainments enjoyed regularly in Stratford in these years belonged to the town fairs in May and September. Stories from folk legends of Robin Hood would be re-enacted by the townspeople. In earlier times the great holy days of the church had also seen performances of religious plays. These developed over the centuries into the great mystery plays which combined religion and local legend and made heroes of those who took the leading parts. They were suppressed as undesirable Catholic propaganda by Queen Elizabeth's officials.

The only plays permitted to be performed in public were those given by the players attached to the household of a great lord. They wore the livery, or uniform, of their lord and patron but they had to support themselves by travelling as a company and performing wherever and whenever they could find an audience. Stratford was visited by several companies of players at various times throughout the 1580s.

Life was not all work. *In Stratford there were two annual fairs. In May there were lusty celebrations for the arrival of summer. Maypoles, cockfights, rope-walkers, beggars, musicians, mock battles, scenes from the life of Robin Hood and buyers and hawkers of all sorts of food and wares celebrated the rush of spring life and the promise of a new harvest.*

Whatever the reality of travelling and performing the players were the most colourful, glamorous and exciting group to be seen in Stratford all year. In their stage roles and stage costumes they not only spoke and performed the play but presented fashion and wit unfamiliar among the people of the countryside.

The May fairs in Stratford like those in other towns probably had pagan origins. It was a day of carnival, including the relatively new fashion of intricate morris dancing by community teams with the hobby horse and the jester. In the working year there were few days given over to entertainment. Most holidays were literally holy days celebrated by church services.

Many theories and suggestions have been offered to account for William Shakespeare's training or profession before he appeared as a player and writer of plays in London. The list of the possible alternatives available to him suggests first that he might have been an assistant to the school master, an usher. Ushers were paid by the master out of his own salary, which in Stratford was a generous £20 a year, but there was little profit in such a job.

Alternatively, he could have tried for a position as a secretary to a rich nobleman. As only boys were educated, only men became secretaries. The only rich nobleman who lived near Stratford was Sir Thomas Lucy, who owned the great estate of Charlecote. Later legends have suggested that the young William offended this magnate by poaching his deer. The laws about killing deer were rigid, the formal deer parks where hunting was allowed were all recorded and Charlecote was not among them.

Writers, and in the sixteenth century this meant poets, might be employed directly by a noble patron. The famous English poet Edmund Spenser was employed as a secretary by the equally famous Earl of Leicester, Queen Elizabeth's favourite. Lesser poets found patrons by dedicating their work to a suitable benefactor. The Queen had more poems dedicated to her than anyone else but rewarded only a few of those who took the trouble to seek her patronage.

Printing was still too new a feature of English life for anyone to make a living from writing books. Besides, all the presses for printing books and all the stationers who sold them were in London. Books were expensive, and often difficult to read. The Bible was the only book widely owned and read by those with sufficient education. Books were an indulgence available only to those with both learning and money.

There was only one real opening for William and at some point he took it. He joined one of the travelling companies as a player, and later wrote and adapted plays for them. It was the most hazardous means of earning a living. From the 1570s no more than a dozen or so acting companies, those who could secure a great lord like the Earl of Leicester as their patron, were licensed to travel the country. An Act of Parliament of 1572 had restricted professional playing to just a few of the bigger companies, and all other travelling groups were banned. When a company reached a new town it had to show the mayor its licence to play. The Queen herself was patron of a company. The small number of such companies of professional players meant that their quality was usually high, and for all the low social status of travelling players there was a considerable oversupply of young men and boys who hoped to join them and become famous players.

Each Christmas the best companies would be summoned to perform at court to entertain the Queen wher-

***The need** to make a living kept the travelling players on the road. Usually about ten actors made a company of players. City authorities, particularly in London, were hostile to all actors. But enrolled as household servants to a noble lord and dressed in the livery of his household they were protected against civil authority. They were servants in name and costume only since they received no wage from their lord. In fact they were independent and commercial, travelling where audiences and money were best.*

ever she was celebrating the Christmas revels. Other sorts of company, musicians and choristers, troupes of jugglers and acrobats, bearwards and other kinds of entertainer travelled too. These were less dangerous than players, who could easily cause trouble with "seditious" or religiously questionable plays. An early Proclamation of Elizabeth's, printed at the outset of her reign in May 1559, called on the mayors of all towns to censor the plays before they could be shown to the townsfolk. This meant an initial performance in the town hall, and the civic accounts all too often list the costs of repairing the hall after a crowd of playgoers had used it. Local mayors always had mixed feelings when a company of players asked leave to perform in the town.

At a great house the performance would normally have taken place in the evening, instead of the daylight or late afternoon performances that the towns enjoyed. Dinnertime and the evening was the leisure time of day for a country landowner and his family and servants, and the day was the travelling time for the players. The com-

Performing a play *at one of the grand country houses along the road was profitable and enjoyable. Those who worked on the estate as well as the indoor servants and staff would crowd into the house and watch the play in the evening. Food, payment and a comfortable bed were the players' reward.*

A page *of the hero's part in the play "Orlando Furioso" by the poet Robert Greene. It belonged to the most famous actor of the day Edward Alleyn, who added his own notes complaining about the length and staginess of the words he had to recite as Orlando, a tragic hero.*

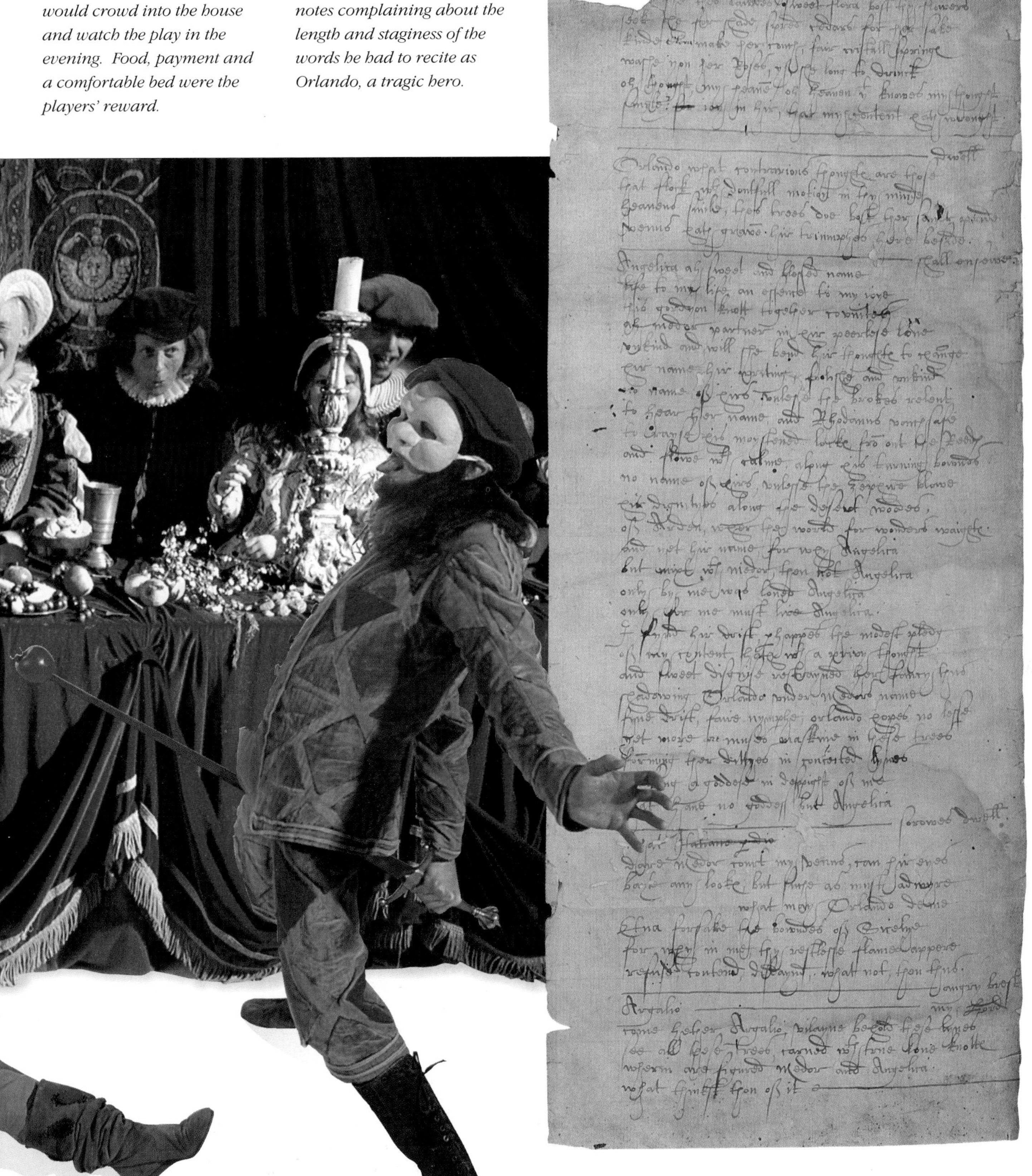

pany would perform on the floor of the great dining hall, in front of the tables where the family might be eating their dinner. They would give their customers a full and lengthy performance, what Shakespeare in *Romeo and Juliet* called the "two hours' traffic of the stage", with all the eloquent poetry, colourful costumes and stage effects that the company could afford to carry with them. Robert Greene's *Orlando Furioso* is an early play that travelled the country. Based on an Italian epic poem, it is a love story in which the hero pins his love poems on a tree (as ten years later Shakespeare was to make his Orlando do in *As You Like It*). Edward Alleyn, who played Greene's original Orlando, enjoyed speaking the extravagant verse laden with classical allusions, though a note in his "part" of Orlando, which is preserved, suggests that he thought some of the verse was a bit extreme and certainly too long.

***The vagabonds** and vagrants of the road may well have had an underworld organisation of their own for 'coney catching', taking the purse or goods of the innocent 'rabbit' in the crowd. Moll Cutpurse was the alias of Mary Frith who inspired two plays "The Roaring Girl"and "Amends for Ladies". Famous in her own life time she spent her seventy years in the Elizabethan underworld. Sentenced to do penance at Paul's Cross for one of many criminal deeds, 'she wept bitterly, and seemed very penitent, but was discovered to have tippled three-quarters of sack before she came to her penance'. Her performance was so arresting that she drew away the congregation from the admonitory sermon on her life being given at the time. She was believed to have appeared on stage herself and was charged with 'appearing in man's attire at the Fortune (playhouse) uttering lascivious speeches and singing bawdy songs while playing the lute'.*

Country houses were communities of their own. The family was always large, covering several generations, and the household was crammed with servants, the estate manager and his land workers. A performance would draw in the entire community, with privileged seating for the members of the family, and perhaps a special place in the musicians' gallery for the household tutors, my lord's secretary, his steward and other senior attendants. The players would get a little money as a gift from the lord, good beds for the night and much better food than they could expect on the road.

The Stratford records for the 1580s list several companies visiting the town. The Queen's Men, formed in 1583, who travelled everywhere in the country, were a conspicuous presence in 1586-7. Other companies, including Lord Berkeley's, the Earl of Essex's, and the Earl of Derby's,

***The Queen** gave orders in 1583 that a company of players be formed under her own patronage. Possessing all the most famous players, The Queen's Men became the leading company for the next five years.*

***Tumblers and leapers** were always successful in attracting crowds before a performance.*

TARLTON

RICHARD TARLTON in the 1570s and 1580s became one of the best known names across England. He was a clown and actor in a company of players, who toured all over England. In the plays he usually took the part of a countryman whose simple directness and ingenuity makes fools of the townsmen he meets. He also had a solo act besides the clown's song and jig that traditionally ended all plays. He would make rhymes on themes suggested by the audience. He was famous for his witty responses. He pleased all audiences even the royal court. The poet Sir Philip Sidney favoured him by taking the exceptional step, unheard of across such a huge social gap between aristocrat and actor, agreeing to be godfather to Tarlton's son.

came every three or four years. The Earl of Leicester's Men may have come to Stratford, especially if, as is widely assumed, they took part in the earl's famous show for the Queen at nearby Kenilworth in 1587. But there is nothing to say which company Shakespeare might have joined. He might have taken the road directly to London instead, to join one of the companies playing there. In the 1580s, though, London was only one of many stopovers for the companies. None of them had a firm or regular place to perform in London. It is most likely that Shakespeare took his chance and joined one of the companies that passed through Stratford.

The professional travelling companies were tightly-knit groups. Usually the team of eight or nine actors, some boys, and a few attendants such as the wardrobe-keeper and the book-keeper, travelled by cov-

***Overleaf** In Bristol in 1578 the crowd trying to get into the guildhall to see the popular comic Richard Tarlton perform was so great that they broke the great iron hinges on the door.*

Queen Elizabeth I

Queen Elizabeth I came to the throne of England in 1558, at the age of twenty five. She was the daughter of Henry VIII and Anne Boleyn. She was intelligent, well educated, a linguist, theologian, musician and poet. She loved pageants, plays, dancing and all forms of hunting. She never married and played her role as a Virgin Queen, using enticement and intelligence in her part. She was fortunate in her ministers, men like William Cecil, and they were fortunate in serving a Queen who promoted herself as the nation personified.

'I know I have the body but of a weak and feeble woman, but I have the heart and stomach of a king, and a king of England too, and think foul scorn that Parma or Spain, or any prince of Europe should dare to invade the borders of my realm; to which, rather than any dishonour shall grow by me. I myself will take up arms, I myself will be your general, judge and rewarder of every one of your virtues in the field.'

She died in her bed after forty four years as Queen. This picture is an idealised progress, supported by her court. The Queen was aged sixty-seven when this picture was commissioned. She appears to be in her twenties, whereas her courtiers are shown at their true ages!

ered wagon, with a few extra horses for the chief actors, who could ride ahead to present their playing licences to the mayor and secure permission to play before the rest of the company arrived. For such visits the leading players would wear their lord's livery as his servants. That made them respectable, and they always hoped that it would make the mayors respectful enough to give them permission to play. Apart from their livery the players gained nothing from their patrons. A letter written by James Burbage and his fellow-players to their patron, the Earl of Leicester, asking for his help to get them a licence to play, specifically assured him that they would be no charge on him otherwise, and they would maintain themselves entirely by performing on their travels.

At some time *between 1585 and 1592 William Shakespeare joined a company of players as a minor actor and maker of plays.*

CHAPTER THREE

To London

When Shakespeare first arrived in London it must have been a revelation to him. It was the fastest growing city in Europe, and within the next fifty years it became the largest city in the world. Rooted beside the Thames since Roman times, where its famous bridge provided the only ready access from Kent and Sussex in the south east across the Thames estuary to Suffolk and Norfolk in the north east. It was the centre of the country in far more than its government. Twenty times the size of the next largest cities, Norwich and Bristol, it was the country's biggest manufacturing centre and its chief port. Every road led to London, and every port and coastal town, from Truro in Cornwall to Newcastle in the north, sent its shipping round the coast to London. London had wealth and industry unsurpassed anywhere in England. More to the point for a newly-arrived actor and aspiring playwright, its human resources and its playgoing population made it also the most likely place in Europe for making money.

London was a well-disciplined and fairly peaceful city. There were occasional riots, including one in Cheapside market over a football match in 1591, and some serious disruptions in 1592 and 1593 when the handicraft apprentices in Southwark rioted over the foreign communities of protestant refugees which they thought were taking work away from the locals. People who went to theatres were routinely accused by preachers of riotous behaviour, but in London itself, apart from some fights between groups of law students and apprentices in the years before 1581, there are few records of any major trouble at any of the playhouses during Shakespeare's years there.

Controlling London's fast-swelling population was none the less a massive headache for successive Lord Mayors. The mayor was elected annually from the leading members of the twelve livery guilds which controlled the

__London Bridge__ was the only bridge from the south of England into the City. In 1592, it was described as 'a beautiful long bridge with quite splendid handsome and well built houses which are occupied by mercants of consequence...'. Not shown, to the right of the picture, was the Great Gateway on which were impaled the heads of executed criminals.

***The streets of the City** of London were crowded just with the number of people who jostled to be inside the walls each day. Tenements wobbled upwards, the buildings leaning together for support, at times completely spanning the road below. Stalls selling all kinds of food and clothing competed with the licensed markets for business. The River Thames was the easiest means of travelling, especially upstream to the City of Westminster. The smell of the river was bad but the smell of the London streets could be overwhelmingly disgusting.*

City's affairs. He had a council like the smaller towns, and City officers whose duties were those of John Shakespeare in Stratford writ large. They controlled trade and business, controlled the various City markets, regulated the annual fairs, and when necessary intervened to keep the peace.

This last activity was never easy. London's population had overspilled its City walls through the preceding centuries, and the Lord Mayor only had official control of the City within the walls itself. The suburbs were where most of the troubles brewed, and there was little the Lord Mayor could do about them. All the entertainment centres, from brothels to bear-baiting arenas and the main playhouses, were located out of the Lord Mayor's reach in the poorer parts on the outskirts of the City. Each parish had its own officers, who kept records of its residents and their births, marriages and deaths, especially from the plague. The parish took care of the poor of its own area, and saw that ditches were kept clear of debris and that the roads were in good condition. Each parish also patrolled its precinct with a night watch. But there was no police force. The magistrates both in the City and the suburbs would convict cutpurses and other robbers, hang or mutilate thieves, expel vagrants when they could lay

'Our unclean sisters' *was how the pamphleteer Thomas Nashe condemned the whores of London to the devil. Bishops could preach but the law was almost helpless against lechery. The evidence of the courts is of comprehensive sexual intrigue through all ranks of society from the level of the Courts and the Great Houses to the merchants, tradesmen, stews (brothels) and the very streets themselves. This vile, and bawdy side of lust flourished just as fruitfully as love was celebrated by the poets and musicians of the day.*

These bare breasted women *advertised their attractions. They persuaded customers to order as much food and drink as possible.*

Life for the disadvantaged *was harsh and often cruel, but a dwarf could pay his way by begging or clowning. In 1554 Edward VI gave the Palace of Bridewell as a refuge for the sick, but it became a prison and a place of punishment for the poor and particularly for prostitutes who were whipped publicly in the yard. The hospital for the insane, known as Bedlam, provided regular entertainment.*

hands on them, and close down any notorious houses, but it was normally up to the citizens themselves to lay the first complaint of any offence. The Middlesex magistrates in the north and the Surrey magistrates in the south did the same, though less rigorously. One of the busiest industries in town was the lawcourts.

Whatever route William Shakespeare took to London from Stratford, by 1592 he had sufficient reputation as a player and playwright to be attacked in the now famous pamphlet of abuse by Robert Greene. Robert Greene, a saddler's son and graduate from Cambridge, lived by writing plays. He was numbered amongst the university wits of London. His work was popular but he lived a drunken and dissolute life. His one attempt to reform had failed, and full of self-pity and reproach he died, destitute.

Beside his attack on Shakespeare, Greene condemned two other of his contemporaries, one of them Christopher Marlowe. His attack put Shakespeare in the company of the most successful playwright of his day. As the outburst of a dying man it also quickly produced a reaction from Greene's friend Henry Chettle. A fellow playwright, Henry Chettle apologised for the abusive pamphlet, saying now that he had seen Shakespeare acting on stage, that he admired his writing, and that "myself have seen his demeanour no less civil than he is excellent in the quality that he professes; besides, divers of worship have reported his uprightness of dealing, which argues his honesty, and his facetious grace in writing that approves his art." This praise was the beginning of a growing chorus in the next years which approved of "gentle" Shakespeare. The word became a discreet way of acknowledging Shakespeare's low social status, saying his manner was gentle even though he was excluded from the gentlemanly rank of the "university wits".

If William stayed in Stratford for the birth of his twins and left immediately they were christened in February 1585 his rise in the theatre as player and writer was meteoric. Within four or five years he had established himself in a double career. He was twenty seven years old. His good fortune was to arrive at exactly the right time.

This opportunity had been forged in particular by the Queen's Men company, formed in 1583. They had the temporary permission of the Lord Mayor to play inside the City of London at a few inns. The Queen's Men was also the company with the greatest number of players, and its success led other companies to increase in size. New plays on a larger scale were necessary and popular. The defeat of the Spanish Armada of 1588 and the triumph over the threat of a Spanish invasion of England

A Groatsworth of Wit bought with a Million of Repentance.

"...Base minded men all three of you, if by my misery you be not warned: for unto none of you (like me) sought those burrs to cleave: those puppets (I mean) that spake from our mouths, those antics garnished in our colours. Is it not strange, that I, to whom they all have been beholding; is it not like that you, to whom they all have been beholding, shall (were ye in that case as I am now) be both at once of them forsaken? Yes, trust them not: for there is an upstart crow, beautified with our feathers, that with his Tiger's heart wrapped in a player's hide supposes he is as well able to bombast out a blank verse as the best of you; and, being an absolute Johannes fac totum, is in his own conceit the only Shake-scene in a country."

This attack was intended to mean that William Shakespeare was an uneducated player who stole the more learned writers' lines to use in his plays. As a player Shakespeare stole the treasures of the poets who like Greene were more properly trained at university in writing and rhetoric. Shakespeare is described as an "upstart crow' dressed in the plumes that the educated poets provided by their words. In Shakespeare's play *Henry VI Part III* the hero, the Duke of York, is taunted by the Queen who had dipped her handkerchief in his son's blood. The Duke's speech of retaliation contains the line "O tiger's heart wrapp'd in a woman's hide!" Just in case the reader had not seen Shakespeare's play, Greene makes his final angry stab at Shakespeare's social pretensions, calling him a "Johannes Factotum", a Jack of all trades, who believed he was the only Shake-scene in the country.

released a flood of anti-Spanish and anti-Catholic plays in the London theatres. Christopher Marlowe had produced the sensational and bloody drama of *Tamburlaine* in 1587. Marlowe stormed the stage successfully again with *Dr Faustus*. Thomas Kyd's *Spanish Tragedy* was another huge success. New and ambitious plays appeared from a whole stable of writers including Robert Greene, George Peele, and Thomas Nashe.

The first record we have of where Shakespeare lived in London does not appear until 1597, when he was fined for not paying his taxes in Bishopsgate. This was a north-eastern suburb between the Tower to the east and Shoreditch outside the northern wall of the City where the two theatres his company was then using were located. Exactly where he would have found his first lodgings we do not know.

***Taverns** were graded according to the price they charged and the quality of their customers. At the lowest level they offered ale and a home to the pickpockets and whores. At the highest level they were eating houses for men of fashion who settled down afterwards to dice and cards. Half way down the scale came the "citizens' ordinary", where for three pennies you ate and drank in the crowded rooms.*

***William Shakespeare** ate and drank in a "citizens' ordinary" and used the light to write in the few hours left in the busy day of a working actor. Surrounded by his fellows there was no peace and quiet from the noise of London life. It was a long way from the quiet seasonal concerns of Stratford.*

He would almost certainly have lived in the suburbs, which were much poorer areas than the City itself, and were therefore much cheaper. The City's dwelling-places were dominated by the citizen-employers, whose houses doubled as their workplaces and warehouses. Great lords owned houses in the Strand and near the Thames and in the rapidly growing sister city of Westminster. The eastern and northern suburbs were where the poorer immigrants and workers lived. Skilled workers and apprentices lived with their employers. House servants of the richer citizens and great lords lived in their masters' houses. All the newcomers, and irregular workers such as hawkers and other street vendors, those who sold market produce, as well as boatmen and the unemployed, all had to live outside the walls. The suburbs, always the poorer parts of Tudor towns, had the usual collection of poor taverns, brothels and slum dwellings that fill the more run-down central parts of modern cities.

He would have found little peace and quiet for his writing in Bishopsgate. Living alone was a rare and expensive luxury and quite abnormal in a society where everyone was expected to live communally. He might have had his own candle, to help him write in the quieter hours at night, but he would have been lucky to get a table for his personal use. He might well have found it cheaper to do his writing in an "ordinary", a tavern where you could buy your dinner, eat and use the table.

Money must have been a constant preoccupation, and not just because of his family back in Stratford. A single sheet of paper cost more than a loaf of bread, and although his fellow-actors were later to claim that in all his writing he had never blotted a word, that does not mean he did not waste any ink or paper. To get a large enough supply of paper just to write out the rough script of a play would have cost him a month's wages as a hired hand in a playhouse.

The first purpose-built playhouse was the Red Lion in Stepney, constructed in 1567. Building the Red Lion encouraged James Burbage, a former player with the Earl of Leicester's Men, nine years later, in 1576, to build the large and confusingly named, Theatre, in Shoreditch, half a mile north of the City gates. In 1599 the Theatre was dismantled, and its framing timbers were used to make the Globe. The Curtain was the second of London's suburban playhouses, built near the Theatre in what was then the green area of Finsbury Fields in 1577. The tradition of flying a flag high above the playhouse to advertise the fact that a play was to be shown appears in the first pictures of London's theatres. A trumpet would also sound from the playhouse roof to tell the spectators, still hurrying out from the city, that the play was about to begin.

__Bull baiting,__ bear baiting and cock fighting were always popular entertainment for Elizabethans. The Queen herself ordered fights to be arranged for her own enjoyment. These animals were expensive so the entertainments were arranged mostly for maximum blood letting rather than death. Spectacular sports were staged. For example, an ape would be set to ride around the pit on a horse. The dogs so excited the horse by snapping at the terrified ape that it would eventually fall into their waiting jaws. There were stars in these arenas too. The bears Harry Hunks and Sackerson must often have set the crowd roaring well within hearing of the neighbouring playhouses.

A Dutch priest, Johannes De Witt, reported from London to a friend back in Amsterdam in 1596 that: "There are four amphitheatres in London of notable beauty, which from their diverse signs bear diverse names. In each of them a different play is exhibited daily to the public. The two more magnificent of these are situated to the south beyond the Thames, and from the signs suspended in front of them are called the Rose and the Swan. The two others are outside the City to the north on the highway that issues through Bishopsgate. There is a fifth, but of different structure, devoted to the baiting of beasts, where are maintained in separate cages and enclosures many bears, bulls and dogs of stupendous size, which are kept for fighting, furnishing a most delightful spectacle."

Two years later a German tourist in London, Paul Hentzner, reported home about his experience of the baiting-houses. The bulls and bears "are fastened behind," he wrote, "and then worried by great English bulldogs, but not without great risk to the dogs from the horns of one and the teeth of the other; and it sometimes happens they are killed upon the spot. Fresh ones are immediately supplied in the places of those that are wounded or tired. To this entertainment there often follows that of whipping a blinded bear, which is performed by five or six men, standing in a circle with whips which they apply to him mercilessly, since he cannot escape them because he is chained. He defends himself with all his strength and skill, throwing down all who come within his reach and are not active enough to get out of it, and tearing the whips out of their hand and breaking them".

By a uniquely lucky accident, we know a lot about what the playing companies were doing in London through the 1590s. Philip Henslowe, an enterprising play enthusiast, built the Rose theatre in Southwark in 1587, as an investment. He was another of the many ex-apprentices who married his master's widow. He joined with a local grocer to invest in building a new playhouse alongside the bear- and bull-baiting arenas a couple of hundred yards to the west of the southern end of London Bridge. His records of the companies who played at his Rose from 1592 onwards have survived, thanks to his son-in-law, the actor Edward Alleyn, who left them to the school he founded, now known as Dulwich College. These records tell an extraordinary tale of frenetic activity, with the companies staging a different play every afternoon, and as many as forty different plays in any one year to satisfy the giant appetite of London's playgoers. Henslowe and Alleyn employed a stable of writers to collaborate in supplying this enormous demand. Henslowe bought most of Marlowe's plays, along with a fair share of all the other new scripts that were now bursting onto London's stages. His various companies playing at the Rose staged at least two of Shakespeare's early plays as well.

The Lord Mayor and council hated professional players, and tried to keep them out of the City itself. He wrote annually to the Privy Council to get them to ban plays. The reasons he gave were chiefly to do with immorality, but also the timing of plays, which drew artisans and apprentices away from their work. "Our apprentices and servants are by this means corrupted and induced hereby to defraud their masters, to maintain their vain and prodigal expenses occasioned by such evil and riotous company, where into they fall by these kind of meetings," he complained to Elizabeth's chief minister Lord Burghley in 1594.

The government, in the form of the Queen's Privy Council, protected the best of the playing companies on the grounds that they were needed each Christmas for

Henslowe

PHILIP HENSLOWE was the son of the Master of the Game in Ashdown Forest in Sussex. In his youth Philip was apprenticed to a wealthy dyer of cloth, and later married his master's widow. This gave him enough money to develop many businesses, including moneylending and pawnbroking. He joined with a local grocer to build the Rose Theatre on Bankside in 1587. In 1592 the Rose was used by Strange's Men, then the best company in London, led by Edward Alleyn. Alleyn married Henslowe's step-daughter, starting a family business which prospered long after Henslowe's death in 1616. He became royal bear-master under King James I. In 1614 he built the Hope as a dual purpose place for staging plays and baiting bears. It became exclusively a bear pit.

Marlowe

CHRISTOPHER MARLOWE was the son of a carpenter in Canterbury. Doing well at school, he was given a scholarship to Cambridge University where he started writing plays, and also made money by spying for the government. His plays, Tamburlaine 1 and 2, *Dr. Faustus* and *The Jew of Malta* took London by storm from 1587 to 1591. They excited playgoers with what Jonson called "Marlowe's mighty line", the wonderfully resonance verse he wrote for his principal players, notably Edward Alleyn. He chose daring subjects. Tamburlaine was an atheist. *The Jew of Malta* satirises all religions. *Edward II* staged the troubles of a homosexual king. Marlowe was in trouble for his atheism in 1593. Before his trial he was killed by an agent of the Privy Council.

Alleyn

EDWARD ALLEYN was born in 1566 in London. He became a travelling player, and the leading actor in the Admiral's Men which brought the first of Christopher Marlowe's famous plays to the London stage. His marriage to Philip Henslowe's step-daughter allied him to London's leading theatre-owner, and by the end of the 1590s he had given up playing for company management. By the 1620s he had made a fortune as an impresario. He used his fortune to establish a school called The College of God's Gift in Dulwich, south of London. The College has preserved his papers, known as "Henslowe's Diary". This records the financial and contractual details concerning the Admiral's Men and other companies working for Alleyn and Henslowe.

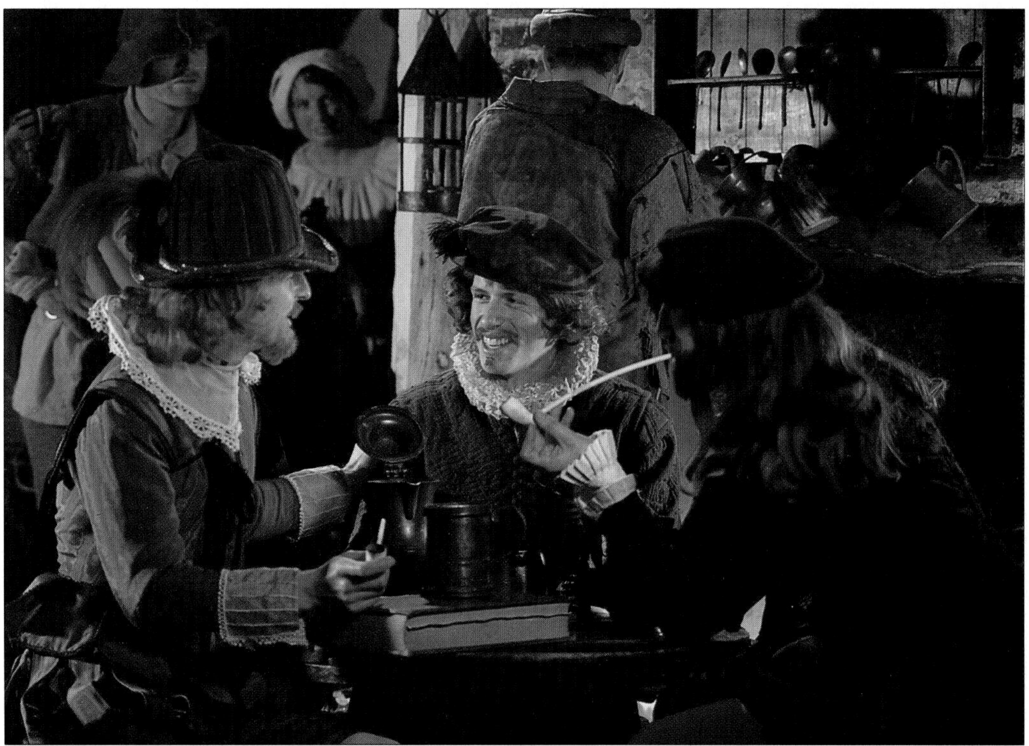

Philip Henslowe *shown here with Edward Alleyn and Christopher Marlowe usually conducted his business in a tavern or even the local stew house (brothel) from which his first playhouse, The Rose, borrowed its name. With his son-in-law he formed the most profitable theatrical dynasty of the age. Money poured in from his other interests, pawn broking, brothels and his animal baiting licences. He profited, too, when he bought the plays of Christopher Marlowe, famous for his atheism, drunkenness and blasphemies as well as the fire and invention of his flowing words on stage.*

Henslowe's Diary

Philip Henslowe's so-called "Diary" was not a diary in the modern sense of a day-by-day written record of events. It was more like a rough account book, with daily entries about his financial dealings with the various acting companies that used his Rose playhouse in Southwark, where he lived. He started it in early 1592, when Edward Alleyn's company was using the theatre, and he was enlarging it to take bigger audiences. It includes all his details of payments for building materials, from wood and nails to plaster and thatch. Alleyn married Henslowe's step-daughter, which cemented their relationship. Many of the "Henslowe papers" are really Alleyn's, and were left by him to his college in Dulwich. That is why, unlike the business papers of all the other playing companies, the records of the companies that performed at the Rose and its replacement the Fortune have survived. The Henslowe papers include all the daily entries for the plays that were performed, their titles, and how much money they brought in. They also give other financial notes, such as how much Henslowe loaned his companies, and what for, his fees for the licensing of the playhouse, his loans to the players to buy playbooks and costumes, direct payments to writers for their plays, some contracts with players who engaged to work for his later companies, and many other papers. They include the "plots" of seven plays, drawn up by the company "book-keeper" (not the company accountant but the keeper of the playbooks), to identify who would be playing which part when they staged the plays, Alleyn's own "part" for one play, letters written to Alleyn by his wife and father-in-law when he was on his travels, and a mass of other correspondence relating to the management of the theatre between 1592 and 1616, when Henslowe died.

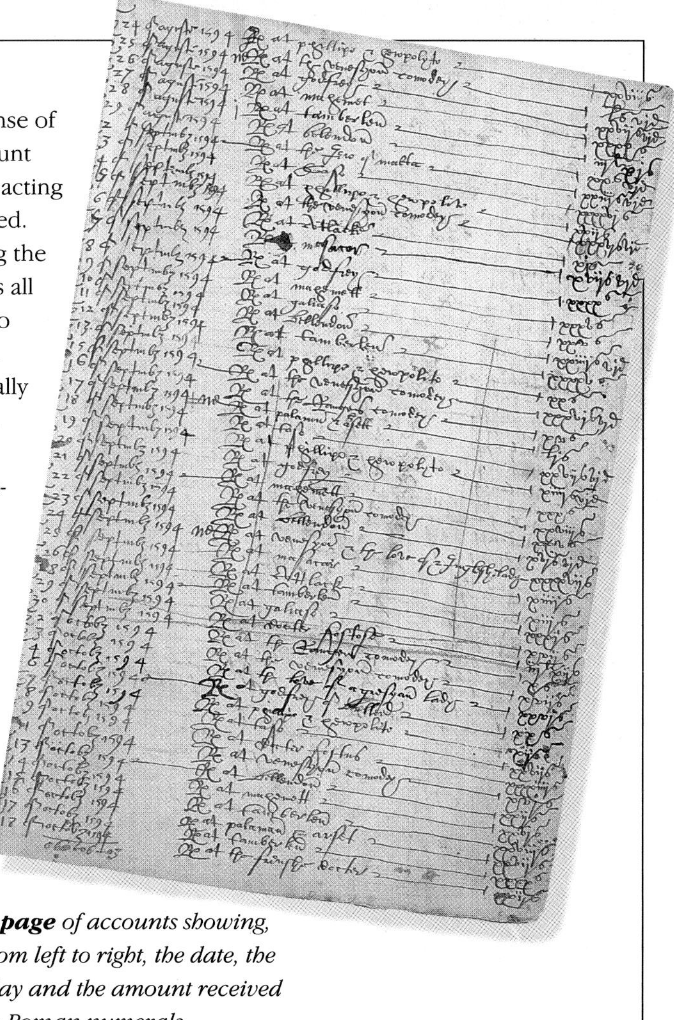

A page *of accounts showing, from left to right, the date, the play and the amount received in Roman numerals.*

Her Majesty's entertainment. The leading companies were licensed "to use and practise stage plays, whereby they might be better enabled and prepared to show such plays before Her Majesty". Nobody suggested that Elizabeth should not be allowed to enjoy some of these idle pleasures once a year. Playing companies were licensed to perform by the Master of the Revels, working for the Lord Chamberlain, a member of the Privy Council, responsible for the monarch's entertainment, and by extension for controlling all the playing companies.

Inside the City, for all the Lord Mayor's attempts to suppress them, some inns were especially redesigned to allow plays to be performed for money, outdoors in the inn's galleried yard. The Bel Savage inn in Ludgate, near Saint Paul's Cathedral, was one of these. These yards were used for a variety of entertainments, or "sports", as they were called. In 1583 some of the Bel Savage's scaffolding collapsed, killing several spectators who were there to see a bear-baiting. The fact that the accident happened on a Sunday gave the preachers lots of ammunition in their attacks on all the godless idlers who went to enjoy themselves at such inns.

Other inns in the City were used in winter, because they made their largest rooms available for performances in wet weather. All these playing places at inns were inside the City limits, and were generally preferred to the outlying playhouse amphitheatres, despite the hostility of the Lord Mayor. He did not secure a ban on playing in the City until 1594.

One really typical example of these early practices by the companies that travelled the country and stopped to play in London whenever they could get a place to play in, can be found in the "frame" device that is a feature of Shakespeare's *Taming of the Shrew*.

The setting of this play is at an inn, the sort of place where the players routinely gave their performances. The hostess of the inn enters quarrelling with Christopher Sly, a drunken beggar. When she goes out to fetch someone to arrest him, Sly falls asleep. A lord returning from hunting finds the sleeping Sly and as a joke has his servants put him the best bedroom and attend him. Next a company of players arrives who offer their play as entertainment to the lord. He instructs them to perform not for him but for Christopher Sly. Sly wakes up and is persuaded he is a lord.

Thus the play that the players perform, about how Petruchio tames Kate, the shrew, becomes a play within the play. The real audience at the inn becomes an audience watching a play staged at an inn for a stage audience. The ease with which all these arrangements fall into place, the lord setting up his fun with Sly, the players arriving at the inn unannounced, their readiness to stage their play for any audience, was a reflection of the real life of the companies of actors up to 1594.

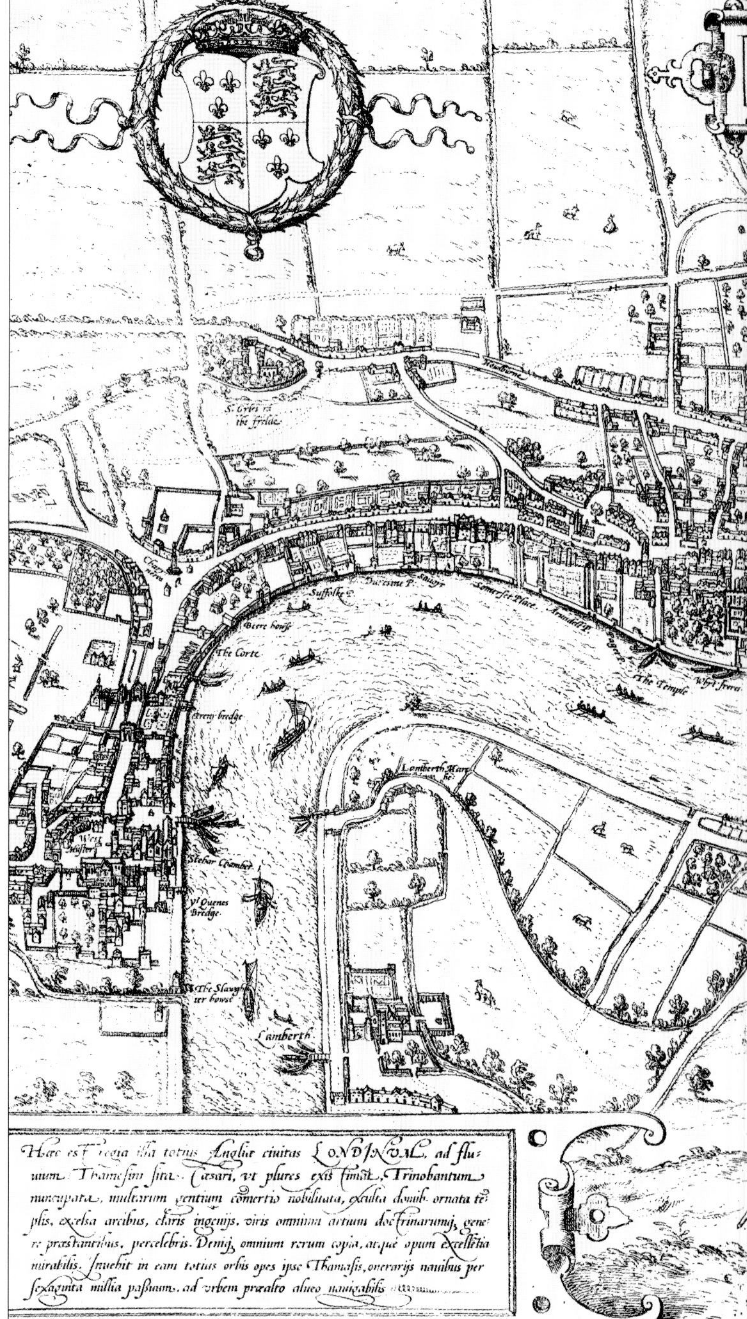

A wholly new market for plays opened in the 1590s. The demand for novelty could not be satisfied, and the Lord Mayor of London was helpless to prevent the playing companies from soaking up the Londoners' cash. For some decades already the universities had been producing more young men highly-trained in the arts of composition than there was employment for in the civil service,

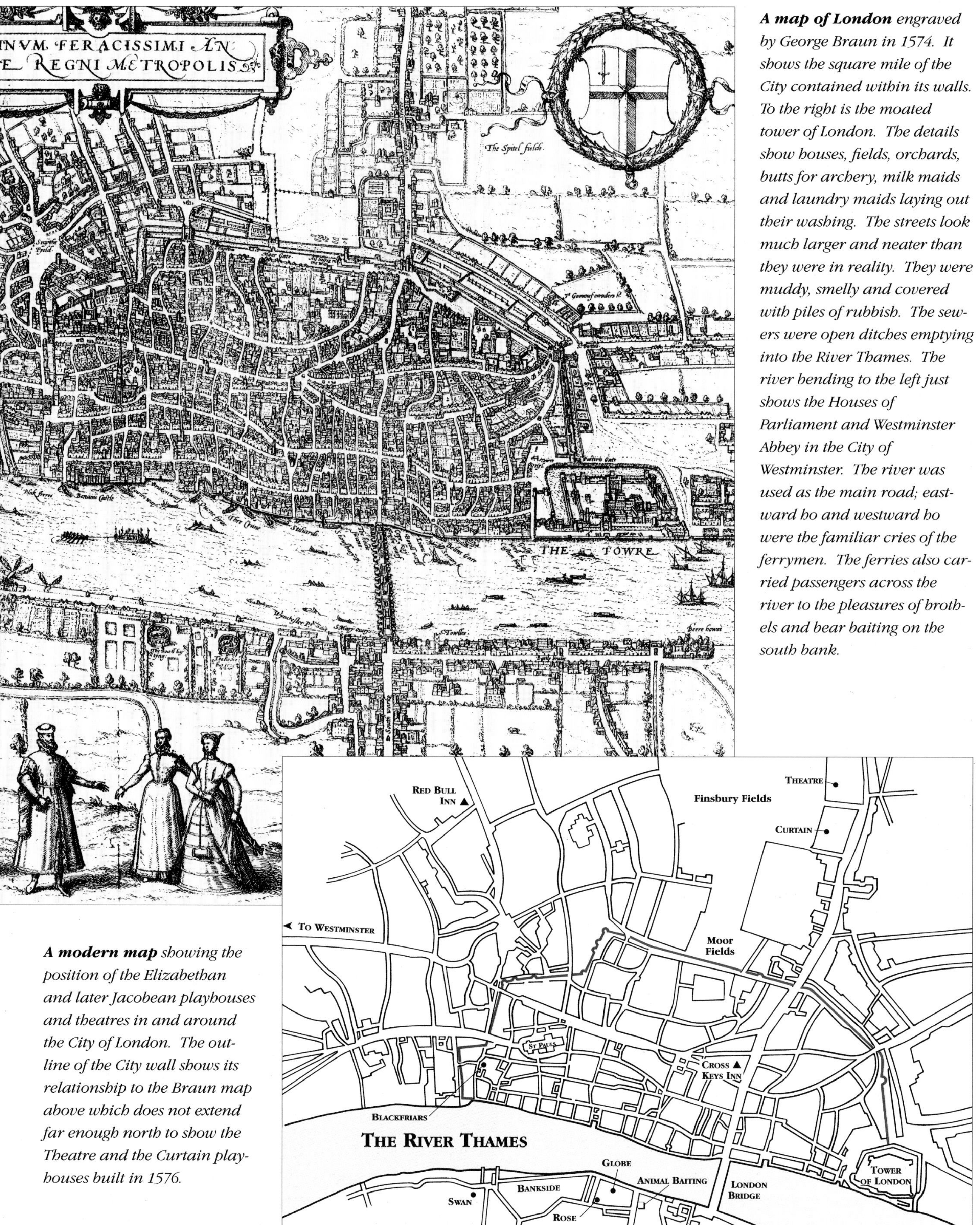

***A map of London** engraved by George Braun in 1574. It shows the square mile of the City contained within its walls. To the right is the moated tower of London. The details show houses, fields, orchards, butts for archery, milk maids and laundry maids laying out their washing. The streets look much larger and neater than they were in reality. They were muddy, smelly and covered with piles of rubbish. The sewers were open ditches emptying into the River Thames. The river bending to the left just shows the Houses of Parliament and Westminster Abbey in the City of Westminster. The river was used as the main road; eastward ho and westward ho were the familiar cries of the ferrymen. The ferries also carried passengers across the river to the pleasures of brothels and bear baiting on the south bank.*

***A modern map** showing the position of the Elizabethan and later Jacobean playhouses and theatres in and around the City of London. The outline of the City wall shows its relationship to the Braun map above which does not extend far enough north to show the Theatre and the Curtain playhouses built in 1576.*

or in the church, or as noblemen's secretaries. The more dissident and the less lucky wrote for the new London market. Many of them tried to find patrons who would pay them for their verses. The less ambitious, who were probably a lot more realistic about their prospects, wrote plays for Henslowe and the playing companies. Some wrote their own compositions. Others joined teams of three or four writers, versifying stories to an agreed plotline. It is notable that the only poets in the 1590s who appear to have made any profit from their writing were the lucky few whose verses were graced with a donation from the man or woman they were dedicated to. The collaborator-playwrights were paid hardly as much as the hired men working in the playhouses themselves.

Robert Greene's outburst marked Shakespeare's arrival as a successful playwright. It was another six years before his name as an attraction to potential buyers began to appear on the title pages of his plays.

William Shakespeare's literary reputation reached new heights in 1593, with his first long poem, *Venus and Adonis*. It appealed not to the serious reader who saw Virgil as the great classical model, but to readers of lighter verse whose taste was for the more accessible and sexy Ovid. This double success, with his plays and his poems, gave him a new set of choices, a richly promising future either as a poet or as a playwright.

At a time when London was all but shut down by plague, William now had the possibility of securing a rich patron, or a host of patrons. The choice carried with it the hazard of perhaps suddenly losing favour, falling out of fashion and being discarded by such patrons. He could be left with the cruel necessity of fawning and writing to please those who might have little beside wealth and social status to justify their patronage. Writing plays offered rather more freedom to write what he pleased, within the limits of what the Master of the Revels might decide to censor, and the daily acclaim of the audiences for whom he would perform. Writing for lords meant an elevated social status, freedom from the daily drudgery of work in the London playhouses, and a highly educated readership for his verse. Writing for public-theatre audiences meant daily but transient praise, and an endless

Shakespeare's comedy, *"The Taming of the Shrew" takes place in a tavern. Here the play is performed in front of a real tavern audience, who are watching a play about a tavern audience, watching a play. In this scene the hero, Petruchio, carries off Kate, the shrew of the title, as his wife before a cheering crowd.*

commitment to working each day in the same place, a long way from his home and family in Stratford. Already famous, he now needed to add fortune to his fame. He chose to continue writing for the stage.

When more than thirty people died from the plague in any one week, the Privy Council would order all theatres to be closed. Any building where large numbers of people might gather and so run the risk of infection, except churches, was closed. Poorly understood as its cause was, the plague terrified people everywhere. It almost always killed its victims, and was known to be highly infectious. As the weather grew warmer, so the risks increased. People who could afford to leave London did so. The Inns of Court, the law sessions and the work of the court in Whitehall itself, all ceased in June and did not resume until September, or later if the plague attack in that year was a bad one. The players suffered most, because closing the playhouses cost them their living. Their compensation was to leave the infested area to take their plays on tour.

Terror at outbreaks of plague was intensified by the fact that most people were convinced they came as a punishment from God.

Our heavenly parts are plaguey sick,
And there such leprous spots do stick,
That God in anger fills his hand
With vengeance, throwing it on this land.

For London the authorities developed an elaborate system of checks, requiring every one of the one hundred and twenty parishes in the London area to draw up weekly lists of the dead, keeping a separate note of those whose deaths came from plague. Each Thursday they gathered lists to check the totals of plague deaths.

London's streets were visibly marked by the plague, as were its victims by the plague-spots or "buboes" on their bodies. The front doors of houses where plague victims were found were marked officially with a standard sheet of printed script and a red-painted cross. Sometimes the cross was burned onto the door so that it could not be erased. The dead were wheeled on carts to large pits on the flanks of the city where they would be buried in heaps. A bell was carried to ring and warn people that the burial carts were coming.

The plague *was understood as a form of divine punishment. It first struck Europe in 1348 and often destroyed whole towns and villages. Most believed it was a judgement delivered from heaven and the only salvation was to flee from an infected area. This was not an option available to the poor. In some of the bad plague years in London, between 1592 and 1594, grass grew in the streets and the citizens were required to burn their rubbish outside their own doors. At other times the rubbish was left to be picked over by crows, kites and of course rats, the carriers of the bubonic plague. Great pits filled with the victims from the great years of plague are covered by the modern City of London, but plague pits are still occasionally uncovered during building works.*

Shakespeare may have stayed in London writing his plays while the plague ban kept the theatres closed. They stayed shut for most of 1593, and there was doubt whether they would ever reopen. The first and only works he ever published himself, written and printed during the long closures for plague, were *Venus and Adonis* in 1593 and *The Rape of Lucrece* in 1594. These two narrative poems, mythical and erotic stories loosely based on Ovid's Latin poems, were relished by every university student and gallant about town.

Venus and Adonis is a superbly elegant and subtle poem. Its immediate appeal was as a fresh English version of the erotic charms that every student found in Ovid's poems. Each stanza had its own eloquent composure, with the story of Venus failing to seduce the reluctant young Adonis having a comic as well as an erotic appeal. In fact it was composed as a subtle send-up of the feelings it was designed to arouse.

THE PLAYS

SHAKESPEARE had almost finished his ambitious first sequence of history plays by the end of 1591. These plays glorified the Queen's ancestors, the Tudors, and also the ancestors of the Earls of Derby whose family name was Stanley. The fifth Earl of Derby, Ferdinando Stanley, called Lord Strange until he inherited the earldom, had a company of players. Because the heroes of the plays are ancestors of Lord Strange it has been suggested that Shakespeare may have belonged to this company as a young man. In the autumn of 1592 Thomas Nashe reported in a book that *Henry VI* had drawn tears from ten thousand spectators. The actor Edward Alleyn probably played the hero, bold Talbot, and must take some credit for the great success of these plays when first performed at the Rose theatre which belonged to his father-in-law Philip Henslowe.

The three *Henry VI* plays, *Parts 1, 2* and *3*, and *Richard III*, are sometimes known as the first "Henriad", like an epic. All four plays celebrate ancestors of the Stanley family; the heroic Talbots of *1 Henry VI*, who fought Joan of Arc, and the Earl of Derby who triumphantly crowns Richmond as Henry VII, the first of England's Tudor kings, at the end of *Richard III*.

Shakespeare's early comedies included *The Comedy of Errors, The Taming of the Shrew, Two Gentlemen of Verona* and *Love's Labours Lost*. Witty comedies about the follies of love, each one did new and very different things with its old "boy meets girl" story. *The Taming of the Shrew*, for instance, deals with what happens after marriage, mocking the standard ending that assumed the lovers would marry and live happily ever after. *Love's Labours Lost* is the most satirical of the early "romantic" comedies.

***Richard Field**, as a fellow from Stratford and a printer, was the obvious choice when William Shakespeare wanted to publish his first epic poem. By the standards of its day it was very well printed with few typographical errors. It is assumed that William proof read his work, a job usually finished when the press was already running.*

She sinketh down, still hanging by his neck;
He on her belly falls, she on her back.

Now is she in the very lists of love,
Her champion mounted for the hot encounter.
All is imaginary she doth prove;
He will not manage her, although he mount her.

The line saying that "all is imaginary" is at precisely the beginning of the poem's second half. The reader excitedly imagining the experience is left with the story of Adonis leaving Venus, and going on a boar-hunt instead. The boar kills him by sheathing its tusk in his groin, and leaves Venus to love him only as the flower which grows out of his blood.

The poem is a masterly showpiece, an exhibition of what the new English poetry could do brilliantly. It uses richly simple similes, like the one offered to describe Venus when she sees Adonis's corpse:

Or as the snail, whose tender horns being hit,
Shrinks backward in his shelly cave with pain,
And there, all smoth'red up, in shade doth sit,
Long after fearing to creep forth again;
So at his bloody view her eyes are fled
Into the deep-dark cabins of her head.

Venus and Adonis was an instant success. It went through sixteen editions in the years up to 1640, and became everyone's favourite, quoted and imitated as a perfect model of its kind. Even more than the plays, this poem guaranteed the high esteem that Shakespeare enjoyed amongst educated men.

Shakespeare kept his Stratford connections alive throughout his London years. For the publication of *Venus and Adonis* he went to Richard Field, the son of a Stratford tanner who was well known to John Shakespeare. Field was three years older than the poet, and had been apprenticed when young to a major London printer with a shop in Blackfriars. Books were bought and sold as bundles of folded pages without a cover. Binding the pages in a leather cover was part of the service offered by the printer more usually than the stationer. It was an easy step from dealing in leather to being apprenticed to a printer in the sixteenth century. The printer was a Huguenot, Thomas Vautrollier, a French protestant refugee from the vicious religious wars which were still running in France. Richard Field finished his apprenticeship and married his master's wife in 1588, within a year of her being widowed. He entered *Venus and Adonis* in the Stationers' Register for his licence to print it on 18 April, 1593. Usually a writer sold his work to a printer rather like an artist sells his painting today. The artist has no say in how the painting is displayed and he is

***Shakespeare's great patron**, Henry Wriothesley (pronounced Rizley), Earl of Southampton and Baron of Titchfield. When the Earl was nineteen years old Shakespeare dedicated both his long poems to him. He was a graduate of Cambridge University at sixteen, enormously rich and self admiring. He was enrolled at the Inns of Court as the final polish to his education.*

***The dedication** to Lord Southampton prefacing Shakespeare's first long poem, "Venus and Adonis". The dedication is written in the courtly style of a poet seeking patronage from a noble lord. The dedication of his second long poem "The Rape of Lucrece" in 1594, addresses Lord Southampton in a more intimate and assured language.*

not paid any more money if it is hung in a house or a public building. William Shakespeare cannot have expected to earn more money from Richard Field, but the care with which the poems were printed meant that probably it was William himself who corrected the proofs for errors.

Field, however, gave up his copyright in the poem too soon to make a great profit from it, selling it after the first two editions to another printer. Field registered Shakespeare's second poem, *The Rape of Lucrece*, on 9 May 1594, and it appeared a few days later.

Shakespeare chose to dedicate both poems to the young Earl of Southampton. Henry Wriothesley was the third earl in the Wriothesley line of the Southamptons. His grandfather had gained his earldom and made his fortune as Lord Chancellor in the last years of Henry VIII, but by the time his son died in 1581 his debts exceeded his assets. Henry was then only eight, and since the family was still strongly Catholic, he was made a ward of Lord Burghley. Burghley, Elizabeth's chief minister, had a collection of wards all of whom he brought up as good Protestants, but who became wild young men.

Henry Wriothesley was eighteen in 1592, and came of age in 1594. At that time his annual income was over £3,000 a year. For the next seven years his annual expenditure ran at more than £5,000, and by the time he was put in the Tower for joining the Essex rebellion, in February 1601, his debts were enormous.

TO THE RIGHT HONORABLE
Henrie VVriotheſley, Earle of Southampton,
and Baron of Titchfield.

*Ight Honourable, I know not how I ſhall offend in dedicating my vnpoliſht lines to your Lordſhip, nor how the worlde vvill cenſure mee for chooſing ſo ſtrong a proppe to ſupport ſo vveake a burthen, onelye if your Honour ſeeme but pleaſed, I account my ſelfe highly praiſed, and vowe to take aduantage of all idle houres, till I haue honoured you vvith ſome grauer labour. But if the firſt heire of my inuention proue deformed, I ſhall be ſorie it had ſo noble a god-father: and neuer after eare ſo barren a land, for feare it yeeld me ſtill ſo bad a harueſt, I leaue it to your Honourable ſuruey, and your Honor to your hearts content vvhich I wiſh may alvvaies anſvvere your ovvne vviſh, and the vvorlds hopefull expectation.*

Your Honors in all dutie,

William Shakeſpeare.

His life in those seven years had been colourful. He challenged the Earl of Northumberland to a duel, and he struck another gentleman in Elizabeth's presence chamber over a game of cards, losing some of his hair in the subsequent struggle. He went to Holland in 1600 to fight a duel with Lord Grey of Wilton. He joined Essex on the Cadiz expedition in 1596, and was his General of the Horse on his disastrous attempt to quell rebellion in Ireland in 1599. Apart from his gambling, much of his income was spent maintaining his own court of sycophants. At the Essex trial in 1601 he said that he had not added much to the rebellion when he joined the conspirators, because: "I had not above ten or twelve men attending me, which was but my natural company."

Largely by accident, by the time he died in 1624 he had become a powerful figure at court and an exceptionally rich man. In 1597 he had seduced the Queen's lady, Elizabeth Vernon, marrying her secretly when she was pregnant, and fled to France. What saved him was his imprisonment for his part in the Essex rebellion. When King James released him and began to give him some of the riches that had once been Essex's, his wife and his steward had already done a great deal to retrieve his fortunes and make his huge estates profitable. He became a quiet force in the political life of the Stuart court, and one of London's first property developers.

The first poem dedicated to him was published in 1591. Written in Latin by John Sandford, one of Burghley's secretaries, *Narcissus* was about the legend recorded by Ovid of the young man who so loved his picture in the water that he fell into it and drowned. Largely a tactful attempt to tell the young earl what he was in danger of, it had little effect. He made himself a patron of scholars like John Florio, the exiled Italian who translated *Montaigne's Essays*, some of the phrases from which Shakespeare mischievously gave later on to Polonius in *Hamlet*, when Polonius is pompously advising his son how to behave when he is away in Paris. Nashe's *Unfortunate Traveller* appeared in June 1593, the dedication saying, "a dear lover and cherisher you are, as well of the lovers of poets, as of the poets themselves". Whether this is simply a reference to Southampton's flock of friends who also loved poetry, or whether it is a hint about the "dark lady" who betrayed the poet of Shakespeare's sonnets with the poet's patron has been a matter of speculation since they were first published.

CHAPTER FOUR

MASTER OF THE REVELS

All play scripts were read and licensed before they were allowed to be performed in public. The duty of censorship was only one of the functions of the Master of the Revels. This jaunty title was first held by Sir Edmund Tilney. A staid and respected figure, he was a distinguished minor courtier. His office was financed by the government to oversee the production of the Christmas entertainments at Court, the revels of his title. Unlike the title, the work was sober and censorial. He had to read all plays to ensure that they contained nothing offensive, treacherous or seditious before the companies could perform them. Criticism of the Queen or her government was not allowed, and was a far more important part of the censor's job than cutting out blasphemy against God or moral offensiveness. A Yeoman of the Revels kept the stock of costumes and properties needed for the Christmas plays and masques. A clerk in the office kept the records of all this for the Master.

Directions for changes to be made to play texts by the Revels office were written in the margin by the clerk. All public performances were licensed, and justified officially as rehearsals for a performance at court. It was the sort of compromise favoured by governments giving them control over the subjects of the plays and saving them money. It also brought money and protection to the playing companies. It became the interest of the Privy Council, the Queen's ministers, to protect the players in London and oppose the Lord Mayor's best efforts to eject them from the City. Their reason for doing so, they always said, was to make sure the Queen's Christmas entertainments would be properly supplied.

It was the task *of the yeoman in the Revels Office to get everything ready for the Christmas plays at court. A tailor by trade, he took care of the extensive Revels wardrobe. Later, as the players came to use their own costumes, the yeoman became a stage manager and organiser.*

Tilney was appointed in 1578 and soon realised that to put on a masque for a single performance at court cost four times as much money as buying the services of a company of players. Since the government paid the Revels Office bills very slowly with a lot of niggling over expenses, he quickly dropped the number of masques commissioned for the court alone, and became the single largest employer of the playing companies.

***To remove blasphemy**, treason and sedition (criticism of God, the Queen, and the State) from the play script was the work of the censor. Censoring the plays kept the Master and his two secretaries well occupied. Shakespeare's play "Richard II" had the scene where King Richard is deposed, missing from the early printed quartos, evidently because the Master cut it out in case the scene incited treason. In this picture Edmund Tilney makes alterations to a new script with Richard Burbage of the Chamberlain's Men.*

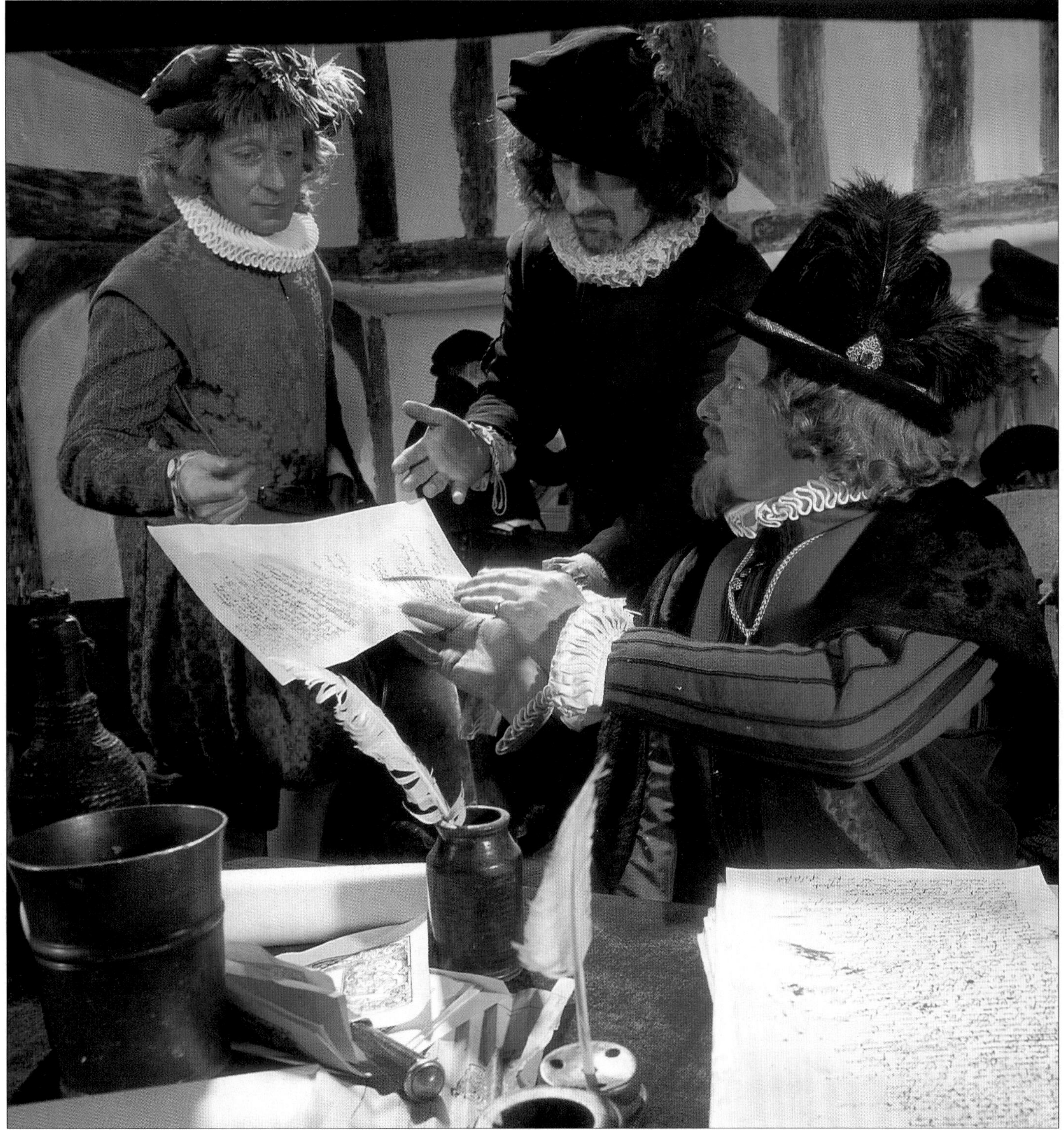

THE BURBAGE FAMILY

JAMES BURBAGE was a player with Lord Leicester's Men. He became a theatrical entrepreneur when he built the first regular open-air playhouse, named the Theatre, in 1576. His eldest son, Cuthbert, trained as an administrator, and his younger son, Richard, as an actor. Richard led the company, which included Shakespeare among the players. Richard, as the foremost actor of his day, took all the leading parts, including Hamlet, Othello and King Lear. James Burbage was an aggressive defender of his property, and Richard was his father's son. On 16 November 1590 the Burbages had a visit from a party with a major grievance. His sister-in-law, the widow of his partner, John Brayne, who financed the building of the Red Lion and later helped finance the building of the Theatre, brought some friends with her to complain that old James Burbage was not paying the money due to her. According to the testimony of one witness, the eldest brother of Edward Alleyn he accused first James and then his wife of abusing the widow from their window, then found "the aforesaid Richard, the youngest son of the said James Burbage there, with a broomstaff in his hand". Another testimony said that the twenty-three-year-old Richard beat one of Mrs Brayne's backers with it, and threatened a second by "scornfully and disdainfully playing with his nose". For such an aggressive family to maintain and manage the most successful company of players is an extraordinary achievement. It cannot always have progressed smoothly, particularly in the beginning. Edward Alleyn fell out with James Burbage so completely in 1591 that he departed never to return. The Burbages offered a triumvirate of theatrical expertise, they sought financial backing from amongst the players and brought about a level of co-operation that was unrivalled.

***Charles Howard**, Baron of Effingham, Lord High Admiral from 1585 and from 1597 Earl of Nottingham, was the patron of the Admiral's Men. His involvement with his players was minimal as they enjoyed the entrepreneurial and management skills of Philip Henslowe and Edward Alleyn. However, the Lord Admiral always supported them in the Privy Council. His wife died in 1603 and he remarried, at the age of sixty seven, a nineteen year old Scottish heiress, an event that invited ribaldry until he died at the age of eighty eight.*

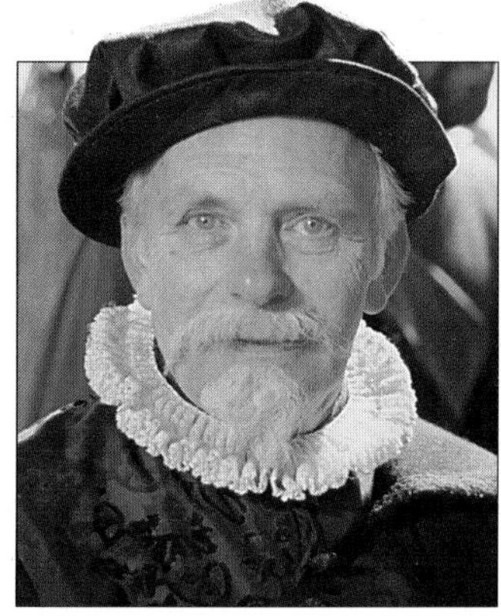

***Henry Carey**, Lord Hunsdon, the Lord Chamberlain, was patron of the Chamberlain's Men, led by Richard Burbage and included Shakespeare. He was the father-in-law of Charles Howard.*

Towards Christmas the Revels Office lived up to its name. Rehearsals took place before the Master, who could pay for much more elaborate costumes than was usual at public performances. His office, and in particular the actors' chamber, heated and lighted for rehearsals, hummed with actors, wig makers, scenery makers, musicians and costumiers.

The Master's master was the Lord Chamberlain, a member of the Privy Council. In 1594 this was Henry Carey, first Baron Hunsdon. His son-in-law was Charles Howard, the Lord Admiral, Tilney's first promoter and also a member of the Privy Council. In May that year, as the plague epidemic which had gripped London for two years eased, the Lord Chamberlain and the Lord Admiral with Tilney's help set up two new companies of players under their own patronage. This gave the two companies a monopoly of London playing, and for the first time a guarantee of security. The status of the two acting companies rose tremendously. Their quality and the quality of their plays rose with them.

The Lord Admiral, Charles Howard, already had a company of players performing in his name for twenty years previous to 1592. Once the plague had dispersed the players to tour for two years it was possible to select the two new companies from the best of the surviving players. It was expedient to form the new companies around established star players and playhouse managers who owned their own playhouse and texts. In spite of these common features in practice the two companies had very different systems of management.

Edward Alleyn was the star of the Admiral's Men, and his father-in-law Philip Henslowe became the company manager. Henslowe also held the licence to run the bear baiting arena, at the Paris Garden. He owned a large

***A diagram** of the Shakespearean company organisation and how it worked.*

Sharers

The eight 'sharers' – controllers of the company policy and practice, buying plays and costumes and managing the company's performances. They chose playbooks, performance schedule, costumes and hired staff.

Theatre Landlord

The theatre landlord (a group of the sharers from 1599 onwards) rented them their place to perform, taking half the takings from the galleries as his rent.

Apprentices

Five or six boy apprentices, generally housed and trained by individual sharers.

Hired men

Ten or twelve hired men, including book-keeper, wardrobe keeper or 'tireman', walk-on players, stage hands.

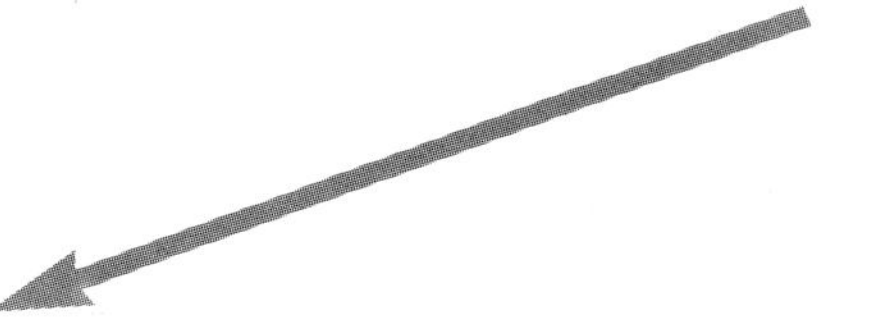

Tireman

The tireman looked after the costumes.

Book-keeper

The book-keeper looked after the play books.

J. Burbage

JAMES BURBAGE was an inventive and enterprising impresario. From his beginnings as an actor with the Earl of Leicester's company, he built both the first durable open-air playhouse in 1576, and the Blackfriars playhouse, the greatest of the roofed theatres in 1596.

R. Burbage

RICHARD BURBAGE, his younger son, was the greatest actor of his time, playing Hamlet, Lear, Othello, and all the other leading roles in Shakespeare's plays. Unlike his father, he was never interested in making money, but worked as an actor till his death in 1619.

Shakespeare

WILLIAM SHAKESPEARE was one of the eight player-sharers in the new company. At thirty he was an actor, the author of the most successful plays and a poet with a good reputation and following in the universities.

Bryan

George Bryan was a player travelling in the Netherlands in the 1580s. Through 1591-4 he acted in Strange's Men, and in 1594 was chosen for the new Chamberlain's Men with Shakespeare. He left acting after a few years, and became a Groom of the Chamber at court.

Heminges

John Heminges was a player with the Queen's Men in the 1580s. In 1593 he joined Strange's Men. He joined the Chamberlain's Men with Shakespeare in 1594. He became the company's financial manager, and co-edited the great Folio edition of Shakespeare's plays in 1623.

Kemp

Will Kemp was the Chamberlain's Men's clown. He left the company in 1599 to dance a morris all the way from London to Norwich, and then, in an even more amazing feat, he danced his way over the Alps into Italy. On his return to London he performed at the Rose playhouse.

Phillips

Augustine Phillips was in Strange's Men in 1593, from whom he moved into Shakespeare's company in 1594. A writer of jigs and a musician, and part-owner of the Globe playhouse. He died in 1605 in Mortlake near London, where he had recently bought a house.

Pope

Thomas Pope performed in the Netherlands in the 1580s, with Will Kemp. He was in Lord Strange's Men in 1593. He joined the Lord Chamberlain's Men in 1594. Playing clown's parts, possibly including Falstaff, he became a part-owner of the Globe in 1599. He died in 1604.

Sly

Will Sly was a Strange's player before becoming a member of the Chamberlain's Men in 1594 with Shakespeare. In about 1605 he became a part-owner of the Globe, and acquired a one-seventh share of the Blackfriars playhouse in 1608. He died later in 1608.

number of play texts but the most popular were those of Christopher Marlowe. Marlowe died in a tavern brawl in 1593 but his work continued to be popular and in performance for the next fifty years.

The Chamberlain's Men had Richard Burbage as their leading player. Their backer was his father James Burbage. His brother Cuthbert was probably their administrator and the company used the original "Theatre" outside the city wall to the north in Shoreditch. They had Shakespeare's plays as their major asset.

The company system was based on team work. It was led collectively by the eight or so "sharers", the leading players, who both invested in and took the profits from playing. The system required the sharers to be on hand for every performance and to take the leading parts.

Henry Carey, first Baron Hunsdon, the Lord Chamberlain, who established the company under his name, died aged seventy two in July 1596. He did not live long enough to appreciate that he had established a unique company, which enjoyed a level of friendship and agreement between the actors equivalent to a modern democratically-run theatre company. As a group it existed for the next forty eight years, growing and developing new fellowships like a single family.

Once the playing companies settled at their approved playhouses in the London suburbs, the memories of constant travel, living out of a waggon and often sleeping in it, began to fade. The players lived in the suburbs near their playhouse, and they worked a day not unlike that of the other artisan workers of the city.

It was the job *of the tireman and his assistants to make and maintain the wardrobe that belonged to the company. As the senior players owned their own costumes the company wardrobe was used to dress special characters, hired men and apprentices. Apparel or costume had status and meaning which was easily understood by the audience. Velvet, worn on stage by characters playing lords and kings, was by law only allowed to be worn outside the theatre by gentlemen and lords. It was extremely expensive. Henslowe invested £20.10s.6d for a 'black velvet cloak with sleeves embrodered all with silver and gold', which was more than a third of the price Shakespeare paid for the second largest house in Stratford. The tireman held a position of great trust and Henslowe had a rule against players leaving his playhouse wearing his costumes.*

Sword fights *on stage had to be as close to reality as possible. The performance was not framed at some distance from the audience but took place literally in front of their noses. Learning to sword fight, an essential education for the sons of gentlemen, was an important skill for a player and required practice.*

Artisans rose early, before dawn, and would expect to get a good two hours' work done before they stopped for breakfast. Since most workplaces lacked artificial lighting, they had to work all the daylight hours. Early rising was important for the actors too, since their new open-air theatres also had to use natural daylight. The mornings were for rehearsals, along with all the work that went with setting up a new play or renewing an old one. The sharers would have long since chosen the week's run of plays, a different one for each afternoon, and the company scribe would have written out the playbills for that day's play. The youths of the company scurried round London pinning the bills on every available post, while the older actors got their costumes ready for that day's show.

The day was a long one, only ending when the costumes for the afternoon's performance had been packed away, and the theatre locked up. The main meal of the day, "dinner" for citizens and players, was between eleven and twelve midday, after which they had no real food until supper in the evening. The gentry ate later, after twelve, before setting off to enjoy the pleasures of the playhouse. That was when the last preparations were being made in the theatre for the day's work. The last hour before performance at 2 pm was occupied by the players skimming through their parts, while the trumpeter practised his notes. The flag was hoisted to announce that a play was ready, and the first-comers of the audience flocked in to get a good place well before the official start.

The demand for new plays in the 1590s meant an extraordinarily intense working schedule for the leading actors. As far as they could, since it was their only source of income, they performed on six afternoons in the week, and they staged a different play each time. They had to have scripts of more than thirty plays in their heads all the time, and the leaders had to memorise up to eight hundred lines for each day's perfor-

***Rehearsals** in the morning reminded the players of their actions over the large area of the stage, their entrances and exits. It helped that in an established company each player specialised in particular parts. A new play had to be rehearsed, and the movements on the stage worked out. The Chamberlain's Men were fortunate in having their best playwright on hand to outline the plot, rewrite a speech and advise from his sources for historical detail.*

Special Effects

The playhouse stage was bright and the curtains colourful. The roof over the stage was painted with sun, moon and stars to signify the sky. Changes of scene or location were registered, often by no more than the entrances and exits of the players. But special effects ranged from false heads which could be cut off, spilling blood, to large scale machinery which lowered gods from the heavens onto the stage. In Shakespeare' s play *Cymbeline*. Jupiter descended on the back of an eagle. Cannons thundered for the death of kings and disastrously in *Henry VIII* when the thatched roof of the Globe was set alight and the playhouse destroyed. Fireworks were frequently used, notably in Marlowe's *Faustus* when devils ran roaring over the stage with fireworks in their mouths, while drummers made thunder in the tiring house and stagehands made artificial lightning in the heavens. Music also contributed to effects, bells rang, drums heralded storms and, with trumpets, conveyed a sense of battle.

mance. More than one new play would be introduced to the repertory every month. It would move in only three weeks from acceptance of the script, to approval by the Master of the Revels, through the copying of the main speaking parts and preparation of the properties and costumes, to rehearsal and first performance.

On some mornings, the roles in a new play the sharers had agreed to buy were assigned to the players. The eight or nine major parts would have been copied out by the company's scribes, and the parts now had to be learned, along with their cue-lines telling them when to speak. The quick learners used any free time they could snatch in the day, while slower learners had to rely on candlelight and privacy in the evenings.

With the licensed "playbook", signed by the Master of the Revels, in his hands, the book-keeper wrote into it the names of the actors he had to get ready for their entrances. With the leading players, he sorted out all the entrances and the properties for each scene, leaving it to their experience to work out how to get offstage again, and how to cope with all the action and movements on stage. Working with the sharers, the book-keeper had already sorted out the patterns of doubling when a player had more than one part. It was the book-keeper's responsibility to see that each player had time offstage to change his costume for each of his parts.

Mostly they used standard techniques. Devils and ghosts made their entries through the trapdoor, kings with their trains entered in state through the wide central opening, and clowns entered by first poking their heads through the central hangings and making faces. Ordinary entries were by one of the two opposed doors on each side of the central opening. The actors had to make special preparations only for such special challenges as the

"A Midsummer Nights Dream" *in rehearsal shows the boys, who play the fairies, take their positions on stage under the watchful eye of Richard Burbage, playing Oberon the fairy king.*

A young apprentice *is transformed by the tireman and his assitant into his first part as a lady's maid. Boys, as young as twelve, played the great female roles in Shakespeare's plays. They learnt to walk in skirts, to gesture and make the audience believe that they were women. Real women were not allowed on stage.*

balcony scene and the final scene at the monument in *Romeo and Juliet*, or the death of Antony in *Antony and Cleopatra*. More routine skills, duelling and flourishing one's hat or (for the boy players) learning a lady's curtsy and using a fan, or the clown's knockabout routines, were matters for individual or small-group rehearsal.

If that day's play was an old favourite, the actors took some of the rehearsal time to revise their parts, and to remind themselves about the action scenes. They also had to check that any special costumes or properties for special scenes, such as boots and spurs if they had to enter from a journey, or a night-cap and candle for night-scenes, were ready to wear. Mostly they provided their own costumes, though if the company had a good resource of especially rich nobleman's wear, that sort of costume was always stored in the playhouse. It was against the law to wear clothing that put you above your class in the street, and no actor was anywhere near the noble rank of the parts he played.

For some of the special effects, the actors had help from the author. Shakespeare must have been consulted for information when his stage directions were insufficient, as they were all too often. In *Henry VI*, for instance, his script specified that Clifford had to enter wounded from battle. The player who took the part of Clifford must have asked how he should appear, because we know that he entered with an arrow apparently stuck in his neck. In Holinshed's *Chronicles of England* which Shakespeare had used to provide the story for the play, it was reported that Clifford was pierced through the neck by an arrow. Only Shakespeare would have that information to hand in the rush of rehearsals. How much more

directing besides this kind of help Shakespeare gave his fellow players each morning we cannot tell. He was only one sharer amongst eight, and could be easily outvoted.

Staging a play was teamwork, and there were severe penalties for anyone who let the team down. Philip Henslowe had a system of severe fines for players who turned up late, or drunk, or who failed to turn up at all unless they had permission from at least three other actors. For all the strain that this intense repertory system laid on the players and their capacity to memorise huge speeches and complex plots, there is remarkably little sign that they had any trouble coping with its demands.

There was a great deal of unease in all the northern European countries about women showing themselves on a public stage, as it was thought to be immoral. Acting was either a matter for school children learning the basic skills of oratory and public speech, which men did not think was proper for women, or for the followers of folk customs, minstrels and professional entertainers, which again were not thought proper jobs for women. Previously in a few of the annual enactments of religious stories in some of the larger towns of England like Chester and Coventry women were allowed in special cases to take part. All these community religious plays were banned under Elizabeth, as forbidden Catholic rituals, so there was no place for women players on the Tudor stages. There is no record of any woman performing publicly on any sort of English stage in the century before Shakespeare, and none after him until the Restoration in 1660, which brought French practices across the Channel. One woman, Mary Frith, did appear on stage in 1610, but she had already made herself a name in London by dressing as a man, wearing a sword. The Henslowe company staged a play featuring her, and she joined the performance in her male clothing, and serenaded the audience. The church court took her to task for indecency.

Edward Alleyn had no children of his own. Like many leading players he treated his boy apprentices as part of his family. He often wrote home to his wife when he was away on tour while the plague shut the London playhouses. His letters to his 'deare sweet mouse' are long and affectionate, full of instructions and advice. For one of his apprentices, John Pyke, nicknamed 'Pig' he wrote a small boy's letter to his mother. John Pyke is not mentioned after this letter and he may have died on tour in 1593. Alleyn himself was too ill to appear when the company reached Bristol.

Boys with unbroken voices were used to portray women. This seemed a logical extension of the basic view that any acting was a deceit, a trick in which a real person pretended to be someone else. School plays used their boys for every part, male and female. It was an extension of this idea which allowed the professional companies to employ young boys for the women's parts.

These boys lived and worked under the protection of a senior actor. The senior players looked after their boys like apprentices, housing and feeding them at their homes when they were in London. It was a kind of apprenticeship, though the player-boys had little resemblance to real apprentices. They had to have unbroken voices, which meant that they were of most use to the company between the ages of ten to fifteen. Real apprentices rarely started their seven-year indentures until they were between fifteen and seventeen. Edward Alleyn, who had no children of his own, behaved like a father to his

Pig's Letter

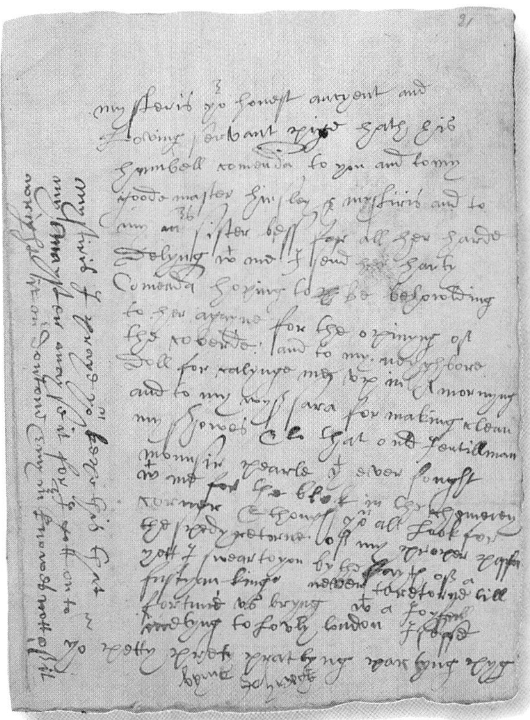

Mistress your honest, ancient and
Loving servant pig sends his
humble comendations to you and to my
good master Henslowe and mistress and to
my mistress' sister Bess for all her hard
dealing with me I send her hearty comendations hoping to
be beholding to her again for the opening of
the cupboard: and to my neighbour
Doll for calling me up in the morning
and to my wife[1] Sarah for making clean
my shoes & to that old gentleman
Monsieur Pearl that ever fought
with me for the block in the chimney
corner & though you all look for
the ready return of my proper person
yet I swear to you by the faith of a
fustian king[2] never to return until
fortune us bring with a joyful
meeting to lovely London I cease
your pretty, pretty, pratling, parleying pig
by me
John Pyke]

1 A joke, possibly referring to his girlfriend.

2 Reference to Edward Alleyn who called himself fustian king in another letter.

THE PLAYS

THE PLAYS written between 1594 and 1603 show Shakespeare rising to the height of his powers. The "middle" comedies, starting with *A Midsummer Night's Dream* and *The Merchant of Venice*, through the wonderful trio of comedies of 1598 to 1600, *Much Ado About Nothing, As You Like It,* and *Twelfth Night or What You Will*, used two exceptional boy actors, one tall and dark and one short and fair, for the leading women's parts in each play, with the result that for the first time the women began to dominate, in word-play and in wit. The combats between Benedict and Beatrice in *Much Ado* created a new model for women, a social revolution in a society which traditionally regarded silence and quietness of voice as the best features of a woman.

In 1595 Shakespeare launched a second series of plays about English history, starting with *Richard II*. Sometimes confusingly called "the second Henriad", it covers an earlier historical period than "the first Henriad". In "the second Henriad, *Henry IV Part I* and *II*, follow the career of the prince who will become king in *Henry V*. The series begins with *Richard II* and contrasts Richard, the rightful king who is ruling wrongfully to Henry Bolingbroke, who seizes the throne and becomes Henry IV, a good king with no right to rule. Henry IV's son becomes king in *Henry V* which ends with the English king's victory against the French at Agincourt. It was written in 1599, while the Globe was being built.

Shakespeare then launched a new series of plays set in Roman history that took theories of leadership and succession into a new political field where there was no hereditary monarchy. *Julius Caesar* was the first play in this series, which Shakespeare left undeveloped, turning instead to write *Hamlet*.

player-boys, particularly John Pyke, called Pig. He wrote a letter for Pig home to Mrs Alleyn when they were on tour together with Strange's Men.

Generally the writers made the women's roles smaller than the men's, although they made them no less demanding. Shakespeare's company had two outstanding player-boys through the period 1596 to 1599, one tall and one short. For them he wrote the parts of Hermia and Helena in *A Midsummer Night's Dream*, Beatrice and Hero in *Much Ado*, and Rosalind and Celia in *As You Like It*. We do not know whether they stayed with the company after their voices had broken. Choirboys usually had to turn to another profession and most of the apprenticed boy actors had to do the same.

The decorums of body language for women, holding a fan, curtseying, and coping with your long and broad skirts, was quite different from the body language of men. The boys with unbroken voices who played the women's parts had to learn a new way of behav-

The jig *was a bawdy dance performed by the company clown dressed as woman. Traditionally it followed the play. The jig may have given the gatherers a chance to collect money from the audience departing from the open yards and market squares of provincial tours. So it was used after every performance even if, as in "Romeo and Juliet", young love lies dead on the stage moments before . In time it was regarded as 'bad taste' and magistrates tried to suppress jigs because of their obscenity in 1612.*

Shakespeare's Sonnets *were published in 1609 without his permission. At this time he was returning to live at Stratford. He had himself published two long poems in 1593 and 1594 which earned him a wide literary reputation as a poet. Poetry was the only form of literature deemed worthy of publication by a gentleman. Although there were rumours of Shakespeare's 'sugared sonnets' circulating among his friends they are not poems he would have wished to be publicly read.*

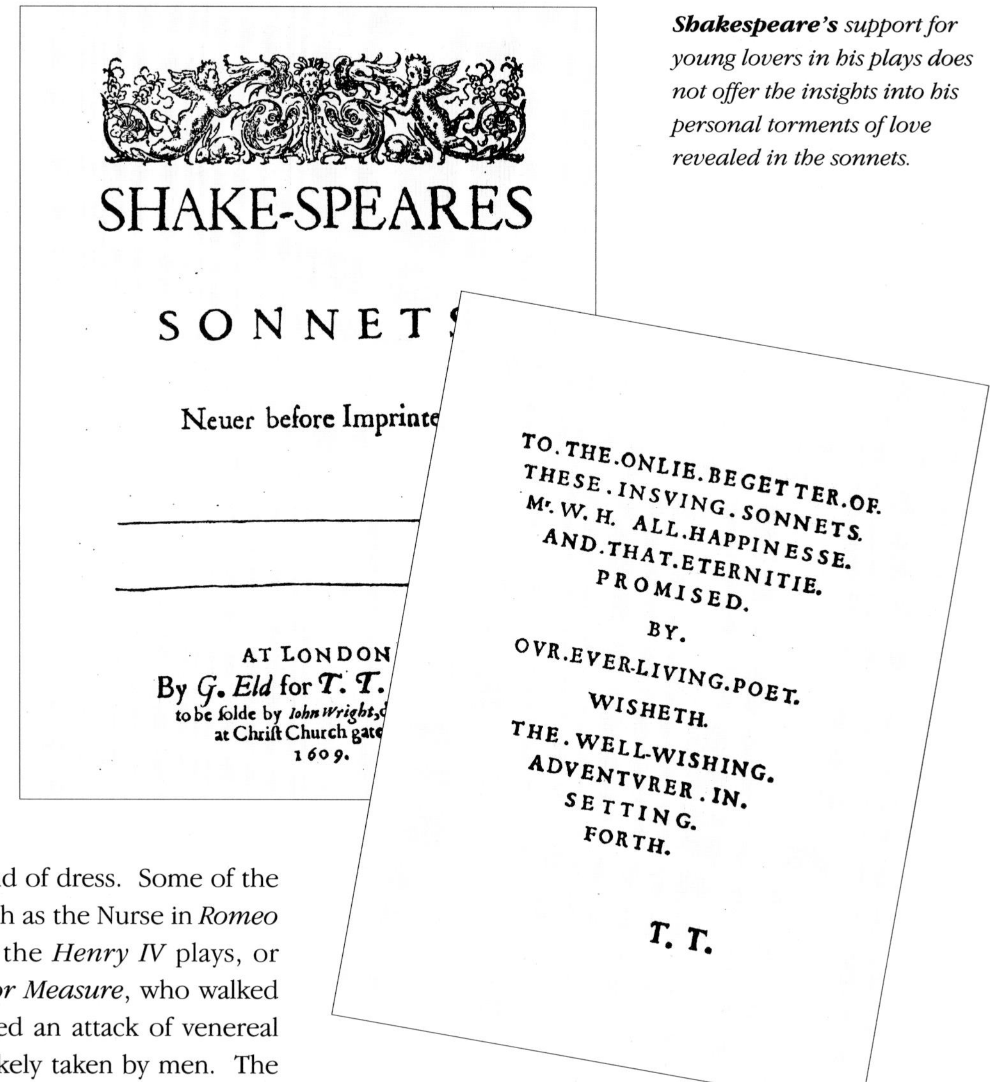

SHAKE-SPEARES

SONNET

Neuer before Imprinte

AT LONDON

By G. Eld for T. T.

to be solde by John Wright,

at Christ Church gate

1609.

TO.THE.ONLIE.BEGETTER.OF.
THESE.INSVING.SONNETS.
Mr. W. H. ALL.HAPPINESSE.
AND.THAT.ETERNITIE.
PROMISED.
BY.
OVR.EVER-LIVING.POET.
WISHETH.
THE.WELL-WISHING.
ADVENTVRER.IN.
SETTING.
FORTH.

T. T.

Shakespeare's *support for young lovers in his plays does not offer the insights into his personal torments of love revealed in the sonnets.*

ing and get used to their new kind of dress. Some of the comic parts for older women, such as the Nurse in *Romeo and Juliet*, Mistress Quickly in the *Henry IV* plays, or Mistress Overdone in *Measure for Measure*, who walked with a comic waddle that signified an attack of venereal disease in her hips, were most likely taken by men. The women's parts in the jig-dances that ended the plays were taken by the same comic men players.

A play always finished with a jig. This was a brief song-and-dance act by the company clown with a couple of assistants that was intended to make everyone go away feeling cheerful. This happened even after the most doleful tragic ending. Thomas Platter's account of his visit to see *Julius Caesar* at the Globe in 1599 includes this note: "When the play was over they danced very marvellously and gracefully together as is their custom, two dressed as men and two as women." The one surviving example of a jig is a rough script called "Singing Simkin". It was probably made up for the Chamberlain's Men's clown Will Kemp, and required the clown and others to sing their lines in rhyming couplets while prancing over the stage in dance rhythm. The jig appealed to the crowd and the general enjoyment of knock-about farce. The lovers are generally the heroes of the moment. Simkin sends the old husband out to buy some sack or sherry, and the final song ends with:

Old husband Yet sirrah you had wit enough
To think to cuckold me.
Wife I jested with him, husband,
His knavery to see.
Sim. But now you talk of knavery,
I pray where is my sack?
Old husband You shall want it in your belly, sir,
And have it on your back.
They beat him off. Exeunt

At this time William Shakespeare was also writing personal poetry. We now refer to this poetry as "The Sonnets" since they were published under this title in 1609. It seems improbable that Shakespeare ever intended them for publication. Francis Meres in 1598 described the circulation of a collection of "sugared sonnets among his private friends" but it is difficult to believe that all of

them were known even in this collection. In the sequence in which they were printed they read like a very personal bundle of letters. Conceivably the entire collection of 154 poems got loose while Shakespeare was packing to return to Stratford after his mother died in 1609 and someone stole a copy and sold it to a printer.

Wonderful and expressive as poetry, they are the only moments when Shakespeare reveals a private life which matches the torments shown in the plays. The use of the personal "I" brings his genius for expression to the muddle, confusion, elation and despair of ordinary life. The sonnet form provides a discipline and frame for what is frequently an outpouring of emotion. Only the fourteen line length of each poem is obvious, the ten syllables to a line and the precision of the rhyming schemes are so assured as to be invisible.

Of the total of 154 sonnets, the first 126 are undoubtedly addressed to the same person. He was a rich young nobleman, probably a lord, and the first twelve encourage him to get married and produce children. They may have been commissioned by the young man's mother. After the first twelve the tone changes and the poet begins to declare his personal devotion to the young man.

Although Shakespeare makes it clear this is not a sexual passion there has been a lot of speculation about whether the "love" that the poet expresses for the beautiful young man was homosexual. There are hints that it came near to a physically-loving relationship, although Sonnet 20 is a witty disclaimer. It says that when Dame Nature was fashioning the young man she intended to make a woman, but fell in love with her and so (for her own sexual reasons) made a man instead by, as the poet says, "adding one thing, to my purpose nothing". He adds a joke about Dame Nature "pricking" him out for her own pleasure. The poems affirm that it was a truly loving relationship, but not a sexual one. Love amongst men friends was openly declared in Shakespeare's time. In *Two Gentlemen of Verona* one of the two heroes is so devoted to his friend that he offers to give him his own beloved lady, although, mercifully, such a noble act of self-sacrifice is rejected.

The so-called "dark lady" poems are among the last twenty eight poems. Unlike the first poems these are certainly not a unified sequence. They are written to more than one woman and on more than one subject. One was written to his wife Anne Hathaway, another is about his own soul, "the centre of my sinful earth", and the final two are thought to be a pun on the Elizabethan cure for sexually-transmitted disease, sweating in hot tubs.

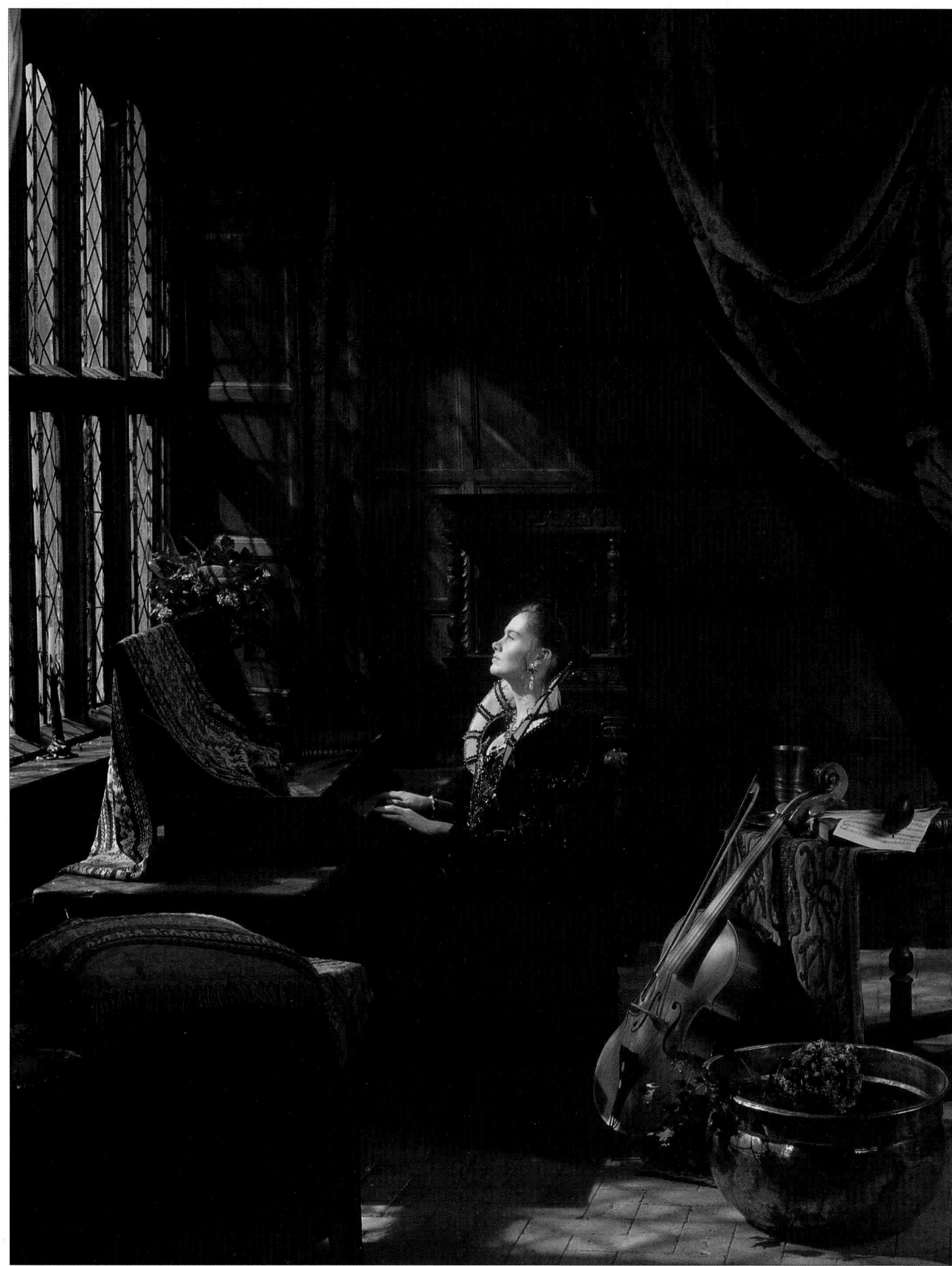

***The Dark Lady** is the name given to Shakespeare's mistress by the Victorians in the nineteenth century. It cleverly supplies an acceptable image suitable for a great poet. Shakespeare was disgusted not embarrassed by his infatuation and lust for his mistress. Her true identity continues to fascinate scholars even before they have established whether she was dark skinned or had unfashionably black hair and eyes. The sonnets give her a literary status that she may not have known socially. They also give her such a dominant presence in the poet's life that completely overwhelms that of his wife Anne Hathaway and indeed other sexual involvements.*

SONNET 116

Let me not to the marriage of true minds
Admit impediments. Love is not love
Which alters when it alteration finds,
Or bends with the remover to remove.
O no, it is an ever fixéd mark
That looks on tempests, and is never shaken.
It is the star to every wandering bark,
Whose worth's unknown, although his height be taken.
Love's not time's fool, though rosy lips and cheeks
Within his bending sickle's compass come,
Love alters not with his brief hours and weeks,
But bears it out even to the edge of doom.
If this be error and upon me proved,
I never writ, nor no man ever loved.

This declaration of constancy in love stands like the Anglican church wedding service that it paraphrases, a denial of the changes that time brings to all human relationships. It uses an image from navigation at sea, the fixed star, whose worth is unknown even when it serves to guide a ship safe into harbour. Each four-line quatrain uses a different image for the constancy in love that the poem defines: the marriage vow, the star, and the constant actor who refuses to act like time's changeable clown. The last couplet sets up a paradox: if this is not true, you cannot be reading it.

Sonnet 116 was misnumbered as 119 in the first printing of "The Sonnets".

Shakespeare's own mistress is the subject of most of the rest of them. The Victorians named her "the dark lady" because he described her hair and colouring as black, the very opposite of fashionable beauty in his day, which was "fair". She is not fair in any sense: colour, beauty or morality, and Shakespeare has the intense emotional pain in knowing that she becomes the mistress of the young man he so admires. His attitude to her ranges from the distant worship of a musician who plays the ironically named stringed instrument, the virginals, to abject sexual disgust. There is self-mocking praise of someone evidently not worth praising, ferocious hatred of the enslaving woman, disgust at the self-deception such sexual enslavement has brought to William himself, and ironic praise of two ageing lovers who lie to one another to conceal their own faults from themselves.

There have been many guesses about the identity of the young man and the "dark lady". The evidence for all these guesses is pretty flimsy. The dates when the sonnets were written are little clearer than the people to whom they were written. Most were composed over a three-year period, and there are verbal resemblances to the *Henry IV* plays which appeared 1596-7. Some of the problems of identity have been made more difficult by the confusions raised in 1609 when they appeared in print, apparently without Shakespeare's permission and with a puzzling dedication to an unknown MR. W. H.

The apparently unsolvable puzzle over the identity of the people who inspired such passions in Shakespeare's life has too often deflected attention from "the sonnets" themselves. As poetry they are some of the most exquisite expressions in English.

"The Sonnets" are a unique window into William Shakespeare's private life in London. At home in Stratford, his son Hamnet aged ten died in August 1596. Unless Hamnet died after a long illness it is unlikely that his father was expecting his death. William had successfully applied to the College of Arms in London to have his own father, John's, coat of arms granted, thereby making him a gentleman. If William paid the fee to the College he also benefited, as his father's son, in becoming a gentleman himself. It was an important step in the ranked society of Elizabethan England. All his fellow players who could elevate themselves seized the opportunity.

Shakespeare scored an immediate success when he created the part of Sir John Falstaff in *Henry IV Part 1*

Elizabeth I *was a great Queen in an age of great statesmen, writers and adventurers. Imprisoned as a child she became Queen of England in 1558. During her reign she personified her nation particularly in the sense of an island fortress. William Shakespeare gave unique expression to the dynamic forces unleashed during her reign.*

"The Merry Wives of Windsor" *is played before the Queen at Christmas. Sir John Falstaff, here dressed as Herne the Hunter, was a great popular success. He combined the worst features of a dissolute old gentleman with wild comedy. The play was an obvious choice for playing at court and rumour suggested that the Queen had demanded Shakespeare write a play about Falstaff in love.*

which the Chamberlain's Men first staged at the Theatre in 1596. Falstaff proved so popular people started quoting his jokes immediately. Sir Toby Matthew, son of the Archbishop of York and a keen playgoer, was citing his lines in a letter by September of that year. Falstaff was the talk of the town in 1596.

But Shakespeare's characterisation of Falstaff drew some less wanted attention too. When first staged he had a different name. Originally he was not Sir John Falstaff but Sir John Oldcastle, a man known to the Tudor historians as a close friend of Prince Hal. In history the Prince had trouble with his friend, because Oldcastle was a Lollard, an enemy of the established Catholic Church, who because of his dissent was hated by the bishops. As a Catholic ruler, the king was forced to persecute him for his religion, and so Oldcastle became a famous rebel. He was famous enough as a hater of the then established Catholic Church to be made one of the Protestants heroes in John Foxe's great book of the 1560s, the *Acts and Monuments*, which was popularly known as Foxe's "Book of Martyrs". Foxe wrote about English men and women whom the Catholic Church had persecuted, and who became heroes and heroines once England finally became Protestant, under Elizabeth.

Shakespeare originally chose Oldcastle for his play from the accounts in Rafael Holinshed's *Chronicles of the History of England*. From soon after his death Henry V had been turned into myth as a heroic king who, like the prodigal son, started enjoying life in dissolute ways, but reformed when he became king and then made himself a model for future ages. With some historical justification, Shakespeare chose Oldcastle for the young prince's dissolute and riotous companion. But he ran into an unexpected difficulty with Oldcastle's living descendant, who happened in 1596 to be the new Lord Chamberlain.

When the Chamberlain's Men's first patron, Henry Carey, died in July 1596, the patronage of the company passed to his son George. But George did not at first follow his father as Lord Chamberlain. The man Elizabeth made the new Lord Chamberlain was Lord Cobham. He was a proud man, and he was also through his mother a descendant of the original Sir John Oldcastle. As the Queen's controller of plays he could insist that Oldcastle's name must be taken out of the new play. Shakespeare had to find a replacement from his own earlier history plays, where Sir John Fastolfe was on record as a coward in Henry V's wars in France. So Sir John Oldcastle in *Henry IV Part 1* was changed to Sir John Falstaff.

It may well be that Falstaff caused Shakespeare some trouble in other ways. The text of *1 Henry IV* suggests that Shakespeare realised quite early on that he had a stage triumph in Falstaff, and so changed his original plan of getting the Prince to vanquish Hotspur and banish Falstaff in the same play. Instead he had to close *Henry IV Part 1* with just the death of Hotspur, and hold back

Falstaff's banishment to a sequel, *Henry IV Part 2*. And that was not the end of it. While writing the fourth act of the sequel, *Henry IV Part 2*, where he took Falstaff off to Gloucestershire and Justice Shallow, he turned aside from his history play for a while to write a new comedy about Falstaff called *The Merry Wives of Windsor.*

Later myth-makers claimed that it was Queen Elizabeth herself who demanded that Shakespeare write a play about "Falstaff in love", and that he did it in only three weeks. This is a doubtful idea, that arose when Shakespeare was a lot more famous than he was in 1596. No records exist of the Queen's opinions about any of the plays she saw at court, and it is extremely unlikely that if she ever did express such a view it would not have been noted at the time. But there is no doubt that Shakespeare did take time off from his sequence of history plays about Prince Hal in order to write *The Merry Wives of Windsor*.

Nothing exists to explain why Shakespeare should have taken Falstaff and Justice Shallow away from the Gloucestershire of *Henry IV Part 2* and relocated them in Windsor. The company's new patron, George Carey, was made a Knight of the Garter in January 1597, and the poet might have expected that his investiture would take place in April at Windsor. In the event Carey was knighted in 1597 not at the usual place for the Garter ceremonies, St. George's Chapel in Windsor Castle, but at the court in London. By then the writing of the play might have been too far advanced to allow any large changes. And in any case, the rival company, the Admiral's Men, had a play of their own about two citizens' wives living in another town by the Thames in Berkshire called *The Two Angry Women of Abingdon*. This matching of the plays in their repertoires by the only two companies licensed to perform in London was not unusual.

The Merry Wives of Windsor was certainly a big success. Falstaff is shown without the Prince, as short of money as ever, trying to improve his fortunes by seducing the wives of two wealthy citizens. It is certainly not a play about Falstaff truly in love, except with money. The two wives in the play are not nearly as attracted to Falstaff as London's playgoers were, and when they find that he has written identical love-letters to both of them they decide to trick and shame him. When one jealous husband returns home while he is there they hide Falstaff in a laundry basket to get him out of the house unseen. They have the laundry basket tipped into the Thames. Falstaff also gets beaten up while dressed as a woman. The final act exposes his deceptions in public.

Even if Queen Elizabeth did not order Shakespeare to write a romantic comedy about Falstaff, *The Merry Wives* certainly fitted the bill perfectly, for all Falstaff's spectacular failures as a lover. It would have still been one of the company's first choices of their new plays to offer to the Master of the Revels for the Christmas festivities at court. At heart social allegiance is on the side of good and virtu-

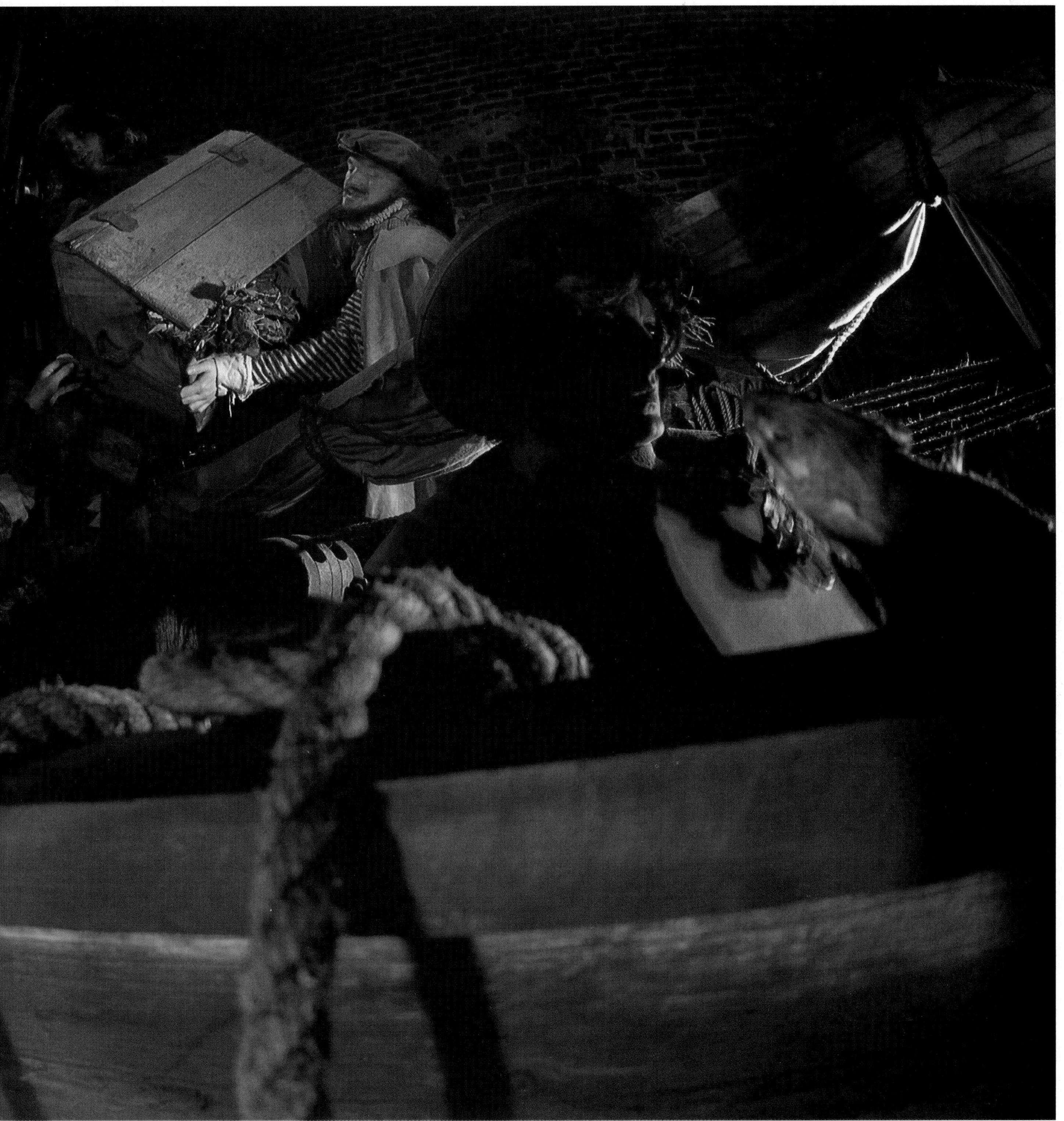

ous citizens against the penniless, idle and selfish gentry of which Falstaff was a prime specimen. It still had its romantic appeal. A young and impoverished gentleman in the play, Master Fenton, who is proclaimed as a friend of the young Prince Hal, outdoes Falstaff by getting away with the prize of a rich citizen's daughter, his true and wealthy love, against the will of both of her parents.

The long day *of the players ends as the hampers of precious costumes are loaded on to a barge, following the evening performance at a grand house in London. The costume, props, tireman and his assistants and probably some of the players will take the easy journey down stream towards their playhouse where the company belongings can be left in the security of their own playhouse watchman.*

CHAPTER FIVE

A MAN OF PROPERTY

By 1596 the Theatre in Shoreditch for which Shakespeare had written *Romeo and Juliet* and all of the Chamberlain's Men's plays up to *Henry IV Part 1* was twenty years old and in need of replacement, as the lease of the land on which it stood was near to its expiry date. James Burbage, the Company impresario, who had built it, had a grand new design. He now planned to replace the Theatre with an indoor hall playhouse that would be better than adapting the largest City inns, and would provide a roof against London's winter weather. He decided to convert part of a building in the Blackfriars, a group of old monastic buildings, into a new playhouse. The old upper frater or room, comprising a large part of this great building complex, had been used for a succession of meetings of Parliament in previous centuries, and for the Vatican's enquiry into Henry VIII's divorce. The Office of the Revels and its storehouses were nearby, in the same precinct. Its size and its location must have seemed ideal to old Burbage.

For a professional company permanently to use an indoor playhouse was a bold idea. The open-air playhouses were originally built to imitate the old tradition of performing outdoors in daylight, in town marketplaces or in the yards of city inns. The company's money-gatherers at the town hall door had an easier job than when the company set up its stage in a market-place and the audience

could escape without paying. Inside they could refuse entry to anyone who would not pay. In open market-places the only way of getting money from the audience was to take a hat round. Winter weather always made roofed playing-spaces more advantageous. In London they switched each season. In summer they used the open-air inn yards, where they could crowd more people in, and in winter the inn halls. When the Privy Council set up the two companies in 1594 and allocated them to the suburban amphitheatres, both companies lost the advantage of a roofed winter venue. Burbage's plan was to restore one to his company for all-year use.

But as soon as he had converted the Blackfriars frater into a playhouse, in November 1596, the Blackfriars residents, a wealthy and powerful group of people, petitioned the Privy Council to ban the players from this new playhouse. Their appeal was eloquent about the troubles that would follow from the noise of public plays disturbing the churchgoers, and how the crowds would cause a nuisance in a busy city neighbourhood full of narrow lanes. The petitioners were successful, which was hardly surprising because the new Lord Chamberlain himself, the member of the Privy Council responsible for the playing companies, and George Carey, the company's new patron, both had apartments near the new playhouse. Their success was an utter disaster for the company, because all its resources of cash were now locked up in a building that they could not use. Old James Burbage died soon after. The closure of the Theatre followed when its twenty-one-year lease expired in April 1597 and forced the company to shift to the nearby Curtain amphitheatre.

Fortunately for the Burbage brothers the Blackfriars playhouse, without alterations, found a tenant. In 1599 the choirmasters of St. Paul's and the Chapel Royal turned some of the skills of their choristers to profit by producing plays, and charging admission for them. In 1600 the Children of the Chapel Royal started performing at the Blackfriars theatre. At first these boy groups were tolerated much more readily than the adult companies. The boys made less noise than the adults, they played only at indoor theatres, and they performed once a week instead of every day. They were also thought of as socially superior to the common players, since they could claim to be

Wenceslaus Hollar, *an engraver from Prague, accurately recorded, in meticulous detail, the proportions of the buildings when he drew this map. It was published in 1647, by which time many of the details Hollar recorded had changed. However, it is now regarded as the only accurate drawing of the second Globe, mislabelled as the Beere bayting h, a name which should be attached to the baiting pit labelled and flagged as The Globe. The second Globe was pulled down in 1644. Hollar's view shows it surrounded by large houses and gardens.*

acting only as part of their education, not for money. They were more exclusive, and charged higher prices for their all-seating theatres with a roof. They were advertised as giving "private" performances, not the "public" shows of the adults. Beside the appeal to snobbery, some educated playgoers found that having boys to play adults made the theatre less realistic but more acceptable.

The fashion for the boy companies, who were ridiculed as "little eyases", or young eagles, in *Hamlet*, lasted only a few years. Their once-a-week playing brought in less cash than the adults, and the supply of new boys was soon choked off by the authorities, so the boys slowly grew into adult players. By 1610 the one surviving boy company was a company of "youths", little different from an adult company. Its leading actor, Nathan Field, was twenty-one. Long famous as the Blackfriars boy

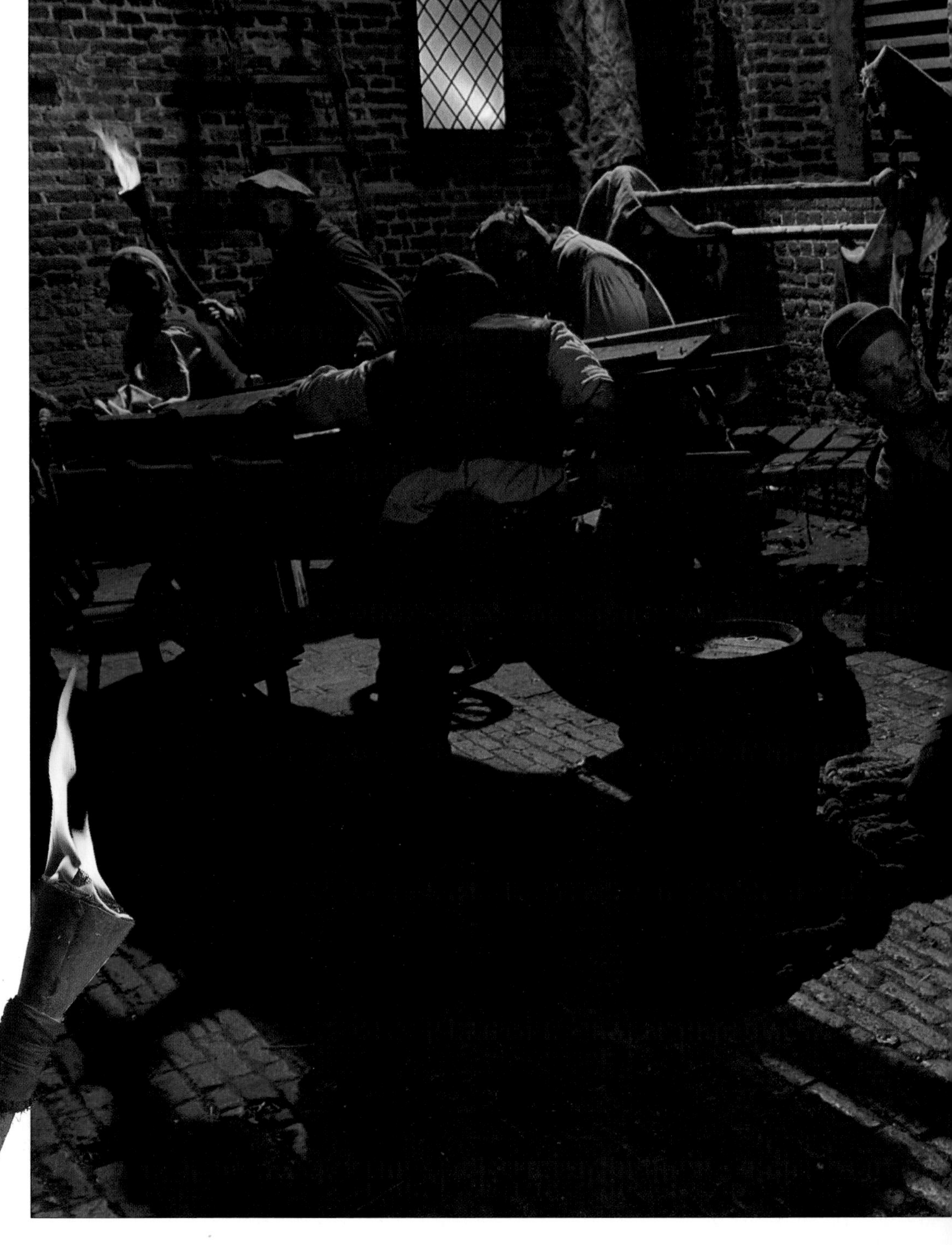

***On a dark winter's day**, the Burbages arranged to steal the great oak timber frames of the Theatre, built at a cost of £700 by James Burbage in 1576. Without these expensive timber frames and the financial and possibly labouring help from the senior players, together with their grim determination, the first Globe could not have been built in 1599.*

company's star actor, he was already writing plays. He eventually joined The King's Men as player and playwright.

The popularity of Shakespeare in comparison with other writers by this time is recorded by Francis Meres in *Palladis Tamia* in 1598. A young student, Meres matched current English writers against their classical models, and found Shakespeare among the best for everything. "As Plautus and Seneca are accounted the best for comedy

Overleaf *The Globe was built in a very short time. It was erected among the market gardens and canals, behind the ale houses, brothels and tenements that lined the south bank. As the huge oak timbers from the former playhouse, the Theatre, were reused there was probably little opportunity to vary the basic amphitheatre plan and no money for extravagant improvements.*

and tragedy among the Latins," he wrote, "so Shakespeare among the English is the most excellent in both kinds for the stage." Writing about the plays that were already well-known on London's stage by 1598, he cites as his comedies *Two Gentlemen of Verona, The Comedy of Errors, Love's Labours Lost,* plus a teasing title, *Love's Labours Won,* which may be either *The Taming of the Shrew* or *Much Ado About Nothing,* or possibly a lost play, *A Midsummer Night's Dream*, and *The Merchant of Venice.* For his tragedies Meres lists the histories *Richard II, Richard III, Henry IV* and *King John*, plus *Titus Andronicus* and *Romeo and Juliet*. He also knew something of what he called Shakespeare's "sugared sonnets among his private friends".

However much money they made from playing as the Chamberlain's Men it was not enough to rescue the company from its troubles at this time. The company sold its more popular playbooks to a printer. Their sales included the most well-known of the recent successes, *Romeo and Juliet, Henry IV Part 1*, *Richard III* and *Richard II*. These side-benefits from the company's success with Shakespeare's most celebrated plays were the first attempts to exploit his new fame as a playwright, to add to his established fame as a poet with *Venus and Adonis*. Two of the newly printed plays had Shakespeare's name on the title page, *Richard III* in its second quarto, and *Richard II* in its third quarto, both printed in 1598.

The money they received for each play went back to the playsharers who had bought it from the playwright in the first place. Today a writer continues to receive payment for his books that are sold by his publisher. In sixteenth century London the printer, who was also often a book seller, made one payment to the owner of the text. For William Shakespeare's plays this was the Chamberlain's Men. Money was the inspiration for publication; gentlemen poets such as Sir Philip Sidney who died in 1586 would not allow their work to be printed or circulated publicly. This hesitation by a gentleman of rank to be identified as an author in print continued after Shakespeare's death in 1616. His plays appeared as quartos, which simply refers to the published size. A quarto was a single sheet of paper about 30cm by 21cm, printed with four pages on each side and folded twice. A complete play resembled a small paperback book. It sold for about six pennies a copy.

To survive, the Chamberlain's Men needed a playhouse of their own, and the two young Burbages had to take their father's place as the company's impresarios, financiers and controllers of the player-sharers' fortunes.

The New Globe Theatre

The original Globe built in Southwark in 1599 was located in Maiden Lane, now Park Street on the south bank, about 90 metres from the River Thames. A careful reconstruction to the original dimensions is nearing completion close to the original site. The new Globe is nearer the river, away from modern traffic noises, and for fire safety it has been provided with larger exits for the audience. Otherwise it is an exact replica. Built with the same variety of oak and deal timbers as the original, it has a yard open to the sky, covered by the same surfacing material as was found at the Rose and Globe sites when they were excavated in 1989. The galleries and the stage cover are roofed in thatch, using the same Norfolk reeds that were found at the site of the Rose nearby on Bankside.

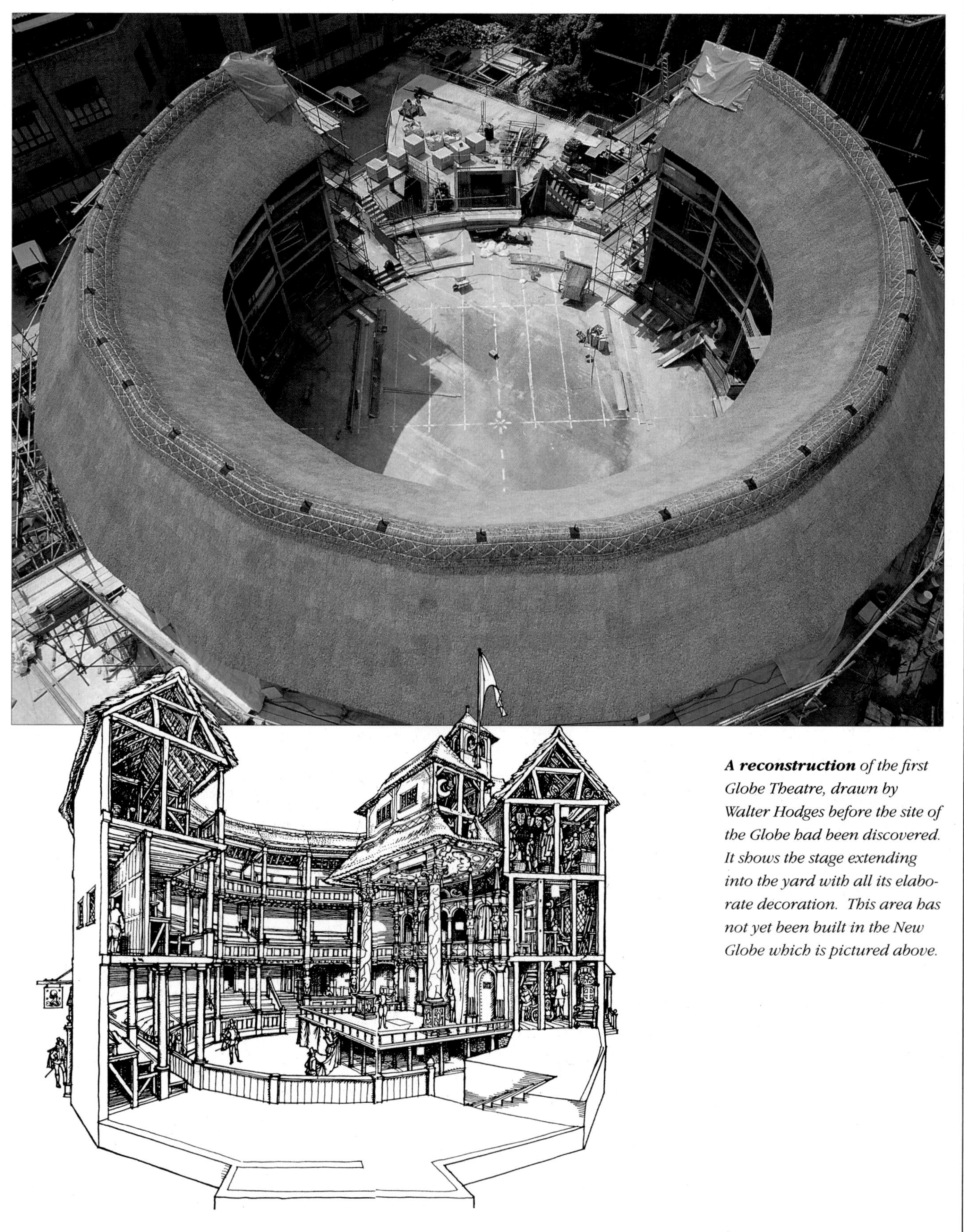

***A reconstruction** of the first Globe Theatre, drawn by Walter Hodges before the site of the Globe had been discovered. It shows the stage extending into the yard with all its elaborate decoration. This area has not yet been built in the New Globe which is pictured above.*

For nearly two years they struggled to renew the lease on the old Theatre. Across the river, Philip Henslowe was still providing the Admiral's Men with his Rose playhouse and ample money to back the activities of his son-in-law Edward Alleyn. A new theatre for the Chamberlain's Men was vital, if they were to match their rivals, and if the Privy Council scheme to allow two companies performing at two fixed theatres was to continue.

The young Burbages must have seen their decision late in 1598 to build the Globe as only a second-best alternative to the lost Blackfriars theatre. They decided to quietly dismantle the Theatre and take its giant frame timbers south across the river to build the Globe. It was technically an act of theft, since ownership of the timbers had reverted to the landowner Giles Allen when the lease expired in 1597. On 28 December when the Christmas season was in full swing and the cold weather was keeping most people indoors they started the work quietly.

Twelve workmen, led by a highly experienced carpenter called Peter Street, tore off the thatch that roofed the galleries and stage, knocked out all the lath-and-plaster that made the infilling for the Theatre's walls, and by knocking out the wooden dowel pins that held the frame together they carefully dismantled the great twelve-inch square oak beams, some of them more than thirty feet high, that formed the frame for the 100 feet diameter polygon. These great beams with their cross-pieces were transported across the Thames to a new site close to the riverside, on a piece of land still known as Bankside, which the Burbages had just acquired on a new twenty-five year lease.

Even though they repossessed the great timber frames, money for fitting out a new playhouse was still a problem. Between them, the Burbages could only afford fifty per cent of the cost, so a radical new scheme to finance the new building was invented. Five of the senior sharers, including Shakespeare, agreed to put up ten per cent each towards the total cost. In fact, when one of the five, Will Kemp, dropped out, the remaining four had to raise their share to twelve and a half per cent each of the total. In this way Shakespeare became a shareholder, owning one-eighth of the Globe as a profitable building which could be rented to his own company of players. Like Richard Burbage and three others of his fellow-actors he became both playhousesharer and playersharer in his company's new playhouse. It proved to be the best decision the company ever made.

The future was now looking richer than ever for those of the sharers who could take money with both hands, as playersharer and housekeeper-owner. Their profit was more than double that of their fellows who remained just players. Shakespeare, taking money from the performances and from the playhouse rents, made the best single investment of a very profitable life when he put up his share to help build the Globe. His combined incomes from the Globe rent and from company playing and from the price he charged for his plays brought him several hundreds of pounds a year, more than ten times what he might have earned had he gained a university degree and become a well paid schoolmaster such as the one under whom he studied in Stratford.

The Globe, being based on a frame of old scaffolding timbers, was built in the traditional form that had already been in use for thirty years in London. It was a big playhouse, more than thirty yards across, and it could accommodate more than three thousand spectators. It had three levels of galleries, thatch roofed, built in twenty

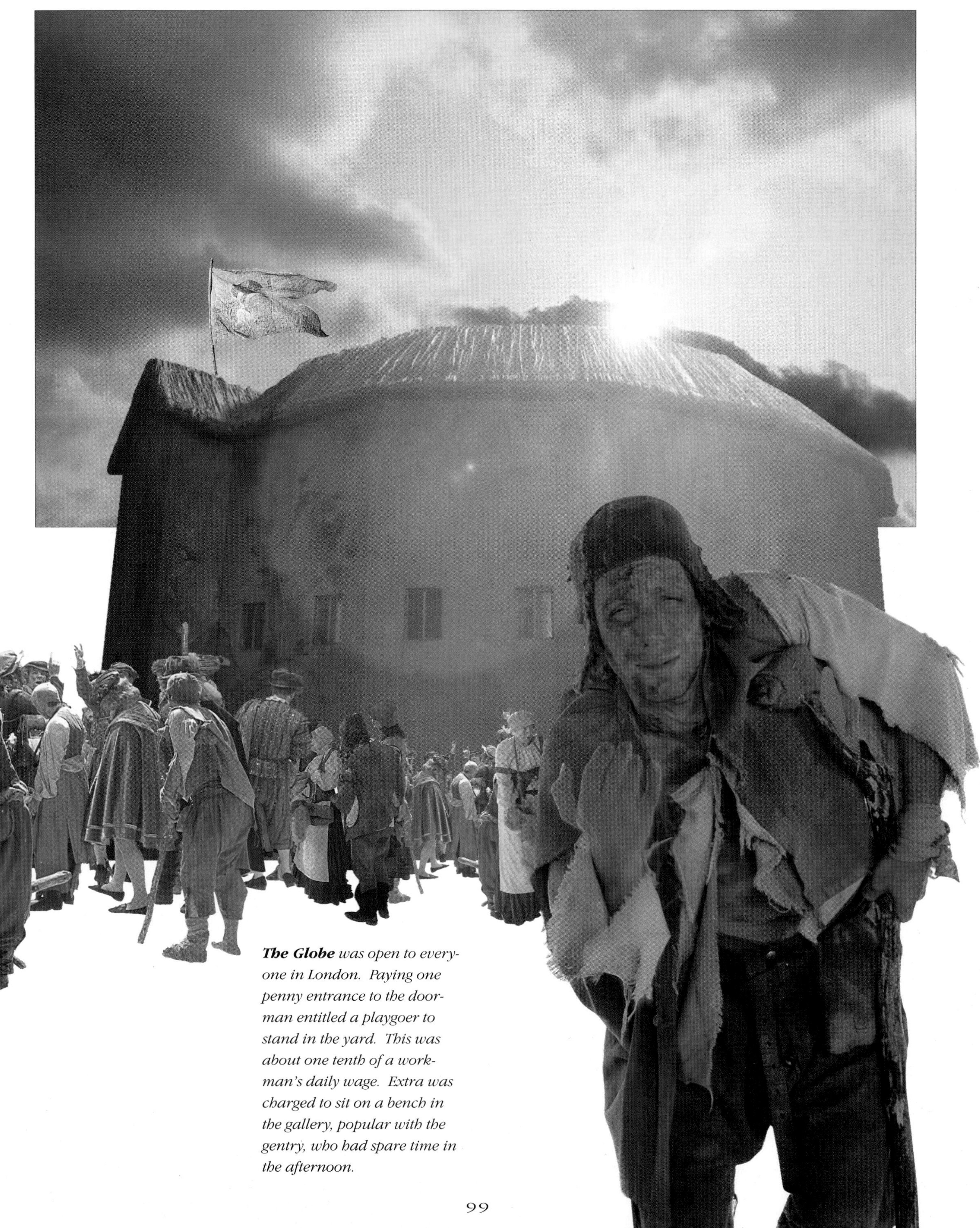

The Globe *was open to everyone in London. Paying one penny entrance to the doorman entitled a playgoer to stand in the yard. This was about one tenth of a workman's daily wage. Extra was charged to sit on a bench in the gallery, popular with the gentry, who had spare time in the afternoon.*

bays surrounding a yard where hundreds of the poorest customers stood around the stage to watch the play. The richer clients sat in the galleries behind the "understanders", compensated for their greater distance from the stage by the roof over their heads and the benches that they could sit on. It was theatre in the round, with a huge platform stage reaching into the middle of the yard, and the players performing at its front, as close as possible to the centre of the "round Globe". The stage itself was at the understander's eye level, five feet, high enough to deter any of the more vigorous members of the audience from trying to climb on stage and join the action.

The actors emerged from a backstage dressing room with two doors flanking a central alcove or "discovery space" fronted by a set of wall-hangings made of cloth of Arras. It was through these hangings that Hamlet stabbed Polonius, before pulling them back to reveal the body. This central opening was also used for grand entrances by kings and formal processions. It was also wide enough to allow large objects such as thrones and beds to be pushed out onto the otherwise bare stage platform. Above the entry doors was a balcony, from which Juliet called to Romeo. Along the same balcony were boxes or "lords' rooms" for the richest customers, who might want to be seen even more than they might want to see the play. Two huge posts stood on the stage to support the "heavens" or "shadow", which protected the players and their expensive costumes from the rain.

Since every performance took place in the afternoon, the whole audience was visible to one another. The famous soliloquies were not spoken as they are in modern theatres, by actors who appear to be talking to themselves. An audience of as many as three thousand in broad daylight, with nearly fifty per cent of them clearly visible on the other side of the stage, needed to be addressed directly. The audiences knew that they were in a theatre much more clearly than we do, when electric light leaves us in the dark in comfortable armchairs. It was not easy to fall asleep when you were watching a play on your feet in broad daylight even on a hot afternoon. You could see the players and they could see you. They talked to you directly. Seeing a play was as strenuous as watching a football match today.

It took about six months to complete the new Globe. While it was going up Shakespeare wrote *Henry V*. The famous prologue, which talks about the theatre as "this unworthy scaffold" and asks: "Can this cockpit hold the vasty fields of France?" was probably written in the expectation that it would open at the old Curtain, though it can be read as hedging its bets, so that the speaker's mock-modesty might be shown up by the splendour of the new venue. *As You Like It* was certainly written for the new Globe, as was *Hamlet*, because both plays celebrate distinctive features of the new theatre.

But the first play that we know opened at the Globe was *Julius Caesar*.

"Julius Caesar" *played at the Globe in September 1599. Although the play is set in ancient Rome, the costumes used were mostly Elizabethan. Audiences did not expect much historical accuracy in costume, although they would have known the story of Caesar's murder.*

Will Kemp *carried on the techniques of the famous clown, Richard Tarlton, playing a country simpleton. He was very successful in the early years of the Chamberlain's Men. By 1599, it seems that the company found Kemp's jigs appealed to a more vulgar type of audience which they hoped to leave behind them when they opened at their new theatre, the Globe, on Bankside. The parts he had played were rewritten for the worldly-wise clown, Robert Armin who replaced him.*

Will Kemp*, pictured far left, made his famous Morris dance from London to Norwich, in eastern England, in nine days while the London theatres were closed during Lent. He published a book about it, "Kemps nine days Wonder," before taking up the challenge of dancing across the Alps to Italy. His replacement, in the company, Robert Armin is dressed like a child in his 'ninnys' costume, on the left.*

A young Swiss student, Thomas Platter, touring the known world, came to London in 1599. After doing the usual tourist things, such as getting a look at the Queen and going to a bear-baiting, he went to see a play on Bankside. At the newly-opened Globe he saw Shakespeare's latest play, *Julius Caesar*. "On 21 September after lunch, at about 2 o'clock, I and my party crossed the water, and there in the playhouse with the thatched roof we witnessed an excellent performance of the tragedy of the first Emperor Julius Caesar, with a cast of fifteen people."

KEMP

WILL KEMP was the last of the famous Elizabethan clowns. He was a popular performer, renowned for his jigs rather than his wit. His roles as stage clown were shortened, over the years, as the plays became more sophisticated. He is thought to have been the performer who was referred to in *Hamlet*, as speaking more than was set down for him, in other words making up his own lines and not using the playwright's text. It has been suggested that his departure from the Chamberlain's Men in 1599, before the Globe opened, was because he had a hand in the piracy by a printer who illegally published a quarto of *The Merry Wives of Windsor*.

ARMIN

ROBERT ARMIN had been a travelling player with Lord Chandos' Men for at least a decade before he joined the Chamberlain's Men in 1600, replacing Will Kemp. He had done solo tours as a performer, as well as playing in his master's acting company. Using the role of court jester rather than Kemp' s country clown, he played Touchstone in *As You Like It*, Feste in *Twelfth Night*, and Lear's Fool, and took over Kemp's original role as Dogberry. A freeman of the City of London as a member of the Goldsmiths' Company, he was the author of prefaces to books, some short verses, and two plays, which advertised his special skills in portraying fools and "ninnies".

A flag, showing Hercules with the globe on his shoulders, flew over the playhouse to say that a play was soon to begin. Over the entry doors was a motto, *Totus mundus agit histrionem*, the whole world is a theatre, which was a Latin tag from the Palingenius of Shakespeare' s schooldays. It is also the opening phrase of that most famous of all speeches from *As You Like It*, melancholy Jaques's "All the world's a stage".

Pictured above its motto, the Globe's emblem showed Hercules carrying the world as a globe on his back. Hamlet refers to it three times in the course of that play, written a little after *As You Like It* for the new venue. When he learns from the ghost of his father that he had been murdered by his uncle, Hamlet clutches his head, and calls it "this distracted globe". It is simultaneously his own head, the burden that Hercules carries on his shoulders, and the distracted world that knows nothing of his uncle's villainy. It is also, though, the world of the theatre, the audience that has come to enjoy some distraction from life's pains. Three times in the play Hamlet contrasts himself to Hercules, the archetypal man of action, comparing the Greek hero's speed and decisiveness with his own inaction.

Hamlet also tells us that the Globe's stage "heavens", the great canopy over the stage which protected it and the actors from rain and sun, was "fretted with golden fire". It would have been brightly painted, like all the stage front, the two wooden pillars that upheld the heavens and all. Above it was a room with a windlass to lower things, sometimes even boy actors, onto the stage. Up in the "heavens" was also where storm effects were produced, thunder noises being made by rolling a lead bullet down a tin channel, or with a drumroll, and fireworks were used to produce lightning flashes.

The staging of the opening lines of *Hamlet* give us a clear indication of how much the words had to carry. The sentries who come on at the opening told the first audiences that the time was past midnight and that it was bitter cold. This was said in the open air at 2 o'clock on a

THE ESSEX REBELLION

ROBERT DEVEREUX, Earl of Essex, grew up as the stepson of the Queen's great favourite, the Earl of Leicester. He left Cambridge University, with a degree, in 1581, aged fourteen. At eighteen, he was General of the Horse in the Dutch wars. He returned to court, not yet twenty, tall, handsome, and charming, and was soon never seen without the fifty-three-year old Queen. The Queen forbade Essex to join an attack against Spain but he went anyway. Elizabeth I eventually forgave Essex but played an odd game demanding repayments of debts while giving him financial favours. She sent him to France to help the French King, fighting the Catholic League. The mission itself was a failure, but his personal bravery shone. On his return, he took advice from Anthony and Francis Bacon. The Bacons were cousins and rivals to the Cecils, who, for two generations, were able and astute secretaries to the Queen. The Bacons extended Essex's political awareness. Essex became a glorious military hero when he returned in triumph having successfully sacked Cadiz, in Spain. His popularity soared, but the Queen was cross and out of pocket for the cost of the expedition. She blamed Essex, but changed her mind and he was restored to his position as her favourite. Francis Bacon warned him to be cautious and submissive to the Queen. But Essex was unwise and there was a famous incident when Elizabeth boxed his ears in public. The row was soothed sufficiently for Essex to take command of the English army in Ireland. He mismanaged his office and made a truce with the rebel Irish leader Tyrone. The Queen imprisoned him. His rebellion against the aged Queen followed and he went to his beheading with undiminished style and glory.

The English expedition *against the Spanish at their port of Cadiz, included the famous English naval commander Walter Raleigh. The Earl of Essex led the forces who were to take Cadiz by land. The expedition was successful but Raleigh refused to wait and attack the Spanish treasure ships returning from the West Indies. As a result the expedition did not return with enough gold and plunder to please the Queen.*

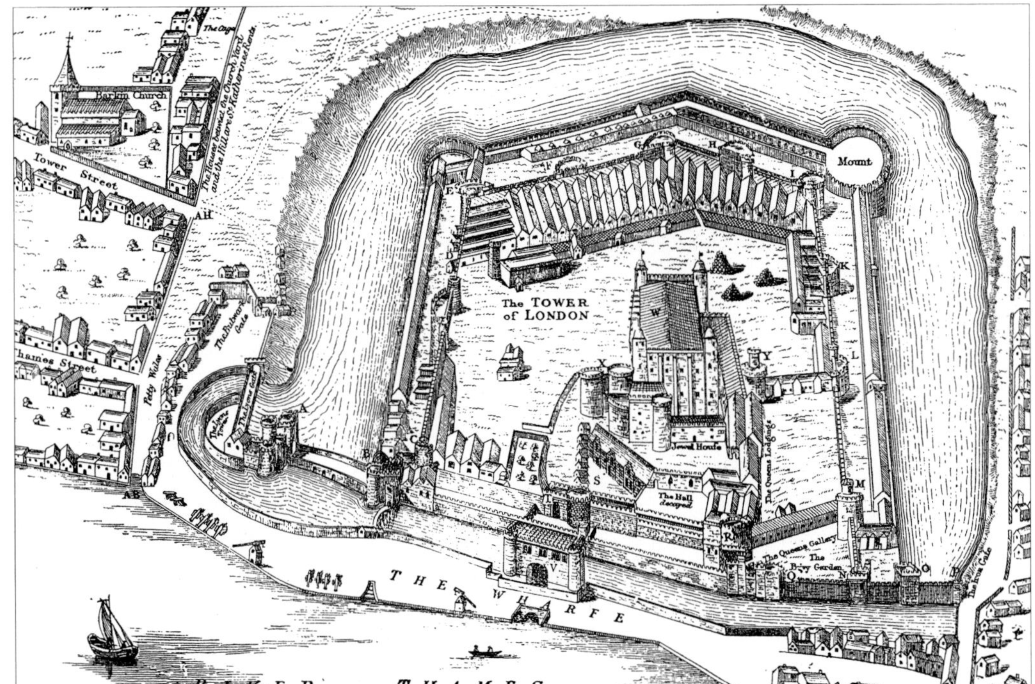

The Tower of London *included within its precincts a permanent scaffold always ready for the execution of traitors. Essex awaited his trial and execution here. He admitted his own guilt: "I think it fitting that my poor quarters which have done Her Majesty true service in divers parts of the world should now be sacrificed at Her Majesty's pleasure". He betrayed his companions not at his trial but afterwards in conversations with a chaplain.*

summer's afternoon. The audiences had to use their imagination to forget the daylight and their visible neighbours in the audience around them. They painted the scene in their imagination by concentrating on what the words suggested to them.

Not long after the staging of *Julius Caesar* and its concluding jig Shakespeare wrote a speech for Hamlet condemning the clown who speaks more than is set down for him. This was written after Will Kemp had left the company and been replaced not by another dancing clown but by a singing jester, Robert Armin. While the Globe was still being finished Kemp sold his share in the new theatre and went off on a famous dance from London to Norwich. He did it on a bet which took him, as he said, "out of the world". He was replaced in the company by Robert Armin. Where Kemp had been a dancer, Armin was chiefly a singer. Shakespeare later wrote the parts of Feste in *Twelfth Night* and the Fool in *King Lear* for him.

In the middle of the cold winter of 1601 in London, a soldier and gentleman called Sir Gilly Meyrick approached the Chamberlain's Men about their playing schedule. He wanted them to perform Shakespeare's *Richard II* on the afternoon of 7 February. It had been a popular play, especially with the more politically alert courtiers when it was written in 1595. It showed Richard II, as the rightful king, guilty of acting as a tyrant by breaking his own laws. His cousin Bolingbroke opposes him and is joined by other discontented nobles. Bolingbroke seizes the crown and makes a better king, although, because he is not the rightful monarch, endless wars follow.

The point of paying the players to perform this play in 1601 was to inspire a group of conspirators, who intended to overthrow the Queen, the following day. The play was a mirror to the leading figures in the rebellion. The rebel Earl of Essex like Bolingbroke felt he could rely on his popularity with the ordinary people of London. He could transform his frustrations as an ambitious, able leader, hindered and imprisoned by an ageing Queen who was losing her authority to grasping, deceiving and flattering courtiers, just like Richard II in the play. William Shakespeare must have known that Dr. John Hayward was still imprisoned in the Tower for writing about Richard II and Bolingbroke in 1599. The company cannot have been unaware of danger when they agreed to perform.

In the event the coup was a disastrous failure. The Londoners all stayed indoors, ignoring the appeals to march with the conspirators. The Earl of Essex, and several of his supporters (though not the Earl of Southampton, who was imprisoned instead), were executed. At Essex's trial the Chamberlain's Men were questioned about their part in mounting *Richard II*. Their spokesman, Augustine Phillips, pleaded that they had objected over the play's age and the small audience they would get for it but they had accepted £2 to perform. They were let off although they were required to play before the Queen on the eve of the Earl's execution.

The only playwright to come near Shakespeare in the

JONSON

BEN JONSON, eight years younger than Shakespeare, was brought up at Charing Cross, north of the City of Westminster. After service as a soldier in the Netherlands, he became an actor and playwright in London like Shakespeare. He had been a good pupil at Westminster School and was regarded as a man of learning, although he was also known for his aggression. He quickly withdrew from the day-to-day work of the stage and attached himself to the rich patrons. His *Every Man in His Humour* was staged by Shakespeare's company in September 1598. Like Shakespeare, he never went to university, but he made himself so famous for his learning that eventually, in 1619, he was awarded an honorary Master of Arts degree, an almost unique commendation at the time, by the University of Oxford. His earlier career was less sedate. His natural aggression led him into a duel with a former fellow-player, Gabriel Spencer, whom he killed in September 1598. He pleaded benefit of clergy, which meant he was let off as a first offence with no more than a brand on his thumb so he could not escape as a first offender again.

esteem of the gentry of their own time was Ben Jonson. He had an on-again off-again relationship with the Chamberlain's Men and with Shakespeare himself. A Londoner a few years younger than Shakespeare, his

Belligerent and touchy, *Ben Jonson was not an easy man to live with or befriend. The details of his life are much better known than Shakespeare's. Rumours of their friendship survive and include William as godfather to one of Ben's children. As playwrights they appeared to have teased each other sharply, but enjoyed and shared ideas as well.*

career also started as a player, and he was still one when he sold them *Every Man in His Humour*, his first great comic success. Legend has it that Shakespeare urged the company to take the play when the majority of sharers did not favour it. It made Jonson's name famous.

One of the jokes in its much more ambitious sequel, *Every Man Out of his Humour*, is about a fool who has a coat of arms with a boar's head on it. The motto suggested as most suitable for such an emblem is "Not without mustard", which of course would have been appropriate for a pork dinner. But it was also dangerously close to the motto that the College of Heralds had awarded Shakespeare's father in 1596, "Not without right". Jonson was poking fun at Shakespeare's social climbing.

Tales were told in later years of the warm and yet combative relationship that the two playwrights maintained. Jonson was compared to a ponderous Spanish galleon, and Shakespeare to a quicker English warship tacking around him and (of course) doing what Drake did to the Armada in the process. That is a colourful image, and may have some truth in it. The two writers certainly cracked jokes against each other in their plays, and they must have enjoyed their working relationship when they were writing for the same company. Some of the plays show signs of a more than casual exchange of ideas. Shakespeare's tragedy *King Lear*, for instance, and *Volpone* which Jonson wrote for the King's Men in 1605 while Shakespeare was writing *Lear*, have some quite remarkable parallels in their imagery and thematic motifs.

By the turn of the century playing, by the professional companies which were now firmly rooted in London's suburbs, was a fast-expanding activity. In 1601 the two adult companies approved by the Privy Council grew to three. The third company at first used the Rose, now abandoned by the Admiral's Men. They had replaced the Chamberlain's Men in the north by building a new theatre, the Fortune, in Golding Lane. Later the Rose company moved to a converted inn to the east of the city, and later still to another inn to the north, in Clerkenwell. At the same time the two boy companies were drawing a lot of attention. The increase to five companies, three of them performing daily, is a clear indication of how fast the demand for plays had grown and it went on growing. The favourites of the last decade, *The Spanish Tragedy, The Jew of Malta, Dr Faustus, Tamburlaine, Richard III*, the Falstaff plays and *Romeo and Juliet*, drew the crowds in their thousands. Law students would quote from Romeo as readily as they had quoted *Venus and Adonis* a few years before. Shakespeare's company, with its new theatre and the riches of his plays, were now unstoppable.

Shakespeare's youngest brother Edmund moved from Stratford to the London suburb on the south bank of the

***Queen Elizabeth I** reigned for 44 years. She inherited her father's throne, following her younger half-brother Edward VI and her elder half-sister Mary Tudor. The Protestants cause in England hung on the thread of her life. The Queen obviously enjoyed the attention of men but to remain single was to remain safely in power. Throughout her life she depended on the guiding hand of her secretary, William Cecil. Her devotion to him on his death bed showed how much she recognised that debt. As her charms grew less, she insisted that the young men, who surrounded her in old age, address her with even greater romantic fervour. She retained her sense of self-preservation and political acumen. Her amazing energies only failed her towards the end of her life.*

Thames at Southwark near the Globe and became a player too, though in other ways he led a different and less successful life than his eldest brother. We do not know what company he joined, though since he was buried in the parish church of St. Mary Overy near the Globe, he may have been taken on as a hired player in the Chamberlain's Men with his eldest brother William. He died aged twenty seven in 1607, and was buried on New Year's Eve at a cost of 20 shillings. This was much more than the cheapest burial, which only cost two shillings. Moreover, Edmund's burial service took place in the morning, not the usual time of later afternoon or evening, which may be another indication that his eldest brother was responsible. A morning burial would have allowed the players to attend the service.

In March 1603 Queen Elizabeth died. She had managed throughout her long life not to name her heir. By this tactic she had kept her courtiers from joining factions in support of different candidates. Elizabeth, on her deathbed, was declared to have named, her cousin, James VI of Scotland publicly, if reluctantly, as her heir. The era of Tudor England had ended.

The Queen *is represented as an idealised figure in this round seal. Her funeral mask is thought to have been painted to represent her as a young girl. She outlived all her favourites and her chief ministers Thomas Walsingham and William Cecil.*

CHAPTER SIX

THE KING'S MEN

KING JAMES VI OF SCOTLAND became King James I of England in March 1603. By April he had arrived in London, although because deaths from the plague were increasing the city's ceremonial welcome had to be postponed. It took place in the following year, when huge ornamental arches were erected throughout London along the route of his procession and carefully crafted speeches of welcome were made. In 1603, though, James had to be content with fitting himself into his new and much richer life in England. By May he was sorting out his pleasures and entertainments. His chief passion was hunting, and on 16 May he issued a proclamation asserting his rights to all hunting lands in the country. On 19 May he thought of the new court's coming season of Christmas revels, and made himself patron of the leading acting company.

The differences between the Tudor court of Queen Elizabeth and the new Stuart regime of her cousin King James I were profound. She succeeded because she knew the value of her advisers and she managed her court and advertised her triumphs as frugally as the public purse demanded, often at her own nobles' expense. James I, by contrast, appeared positively stupid in accepting, as true, the most blatant flattery offered. His inconsistency in uncovering Spanish plots against England and then making peace with Spain confused and alienated many important courtiers. But it was his unchecked extravagance that seemed then, as it does now, an unbalanced lack of common sense and, in consequence, of government. The wars with Spain had been a permanent drain on the public purse. Ten years of bad harvest, at the end of Elizabeth's reign, meant that there were parts of England where half the population was starving. However, money was being made by projectors, such as Philip Henslowe. Projection required money to be invested in a venture, such as trading, shipping or playhouses, in the expectation of receiving it back increased tenfold by the success of the venture. The traditionally rich nobility were finding that they could only maintain their personal wealth if they were given office in the government with its various methods of making money or by joining the projectors. As king, James made no gesture towards the continually increasing population of very poor people. The promotion of unsuitable favourites was another of his shortcomings, but this was simply self-indulgence compared to his inability to spend money within reason.

The Chamberlain's Men, now to be called the King's Men, benefited immediately from James's generosity. They were paid £30 for their first performance before the court in December 1603 at Wilton House seventy miles south west of London. The King was visiting the Earl of Pembroke for the Christmas season to avoid the plague in London. In March 1604 he provided each of the nine named King's Men with four and half yards of red cloth from the Great Wardrobe, so they could wear his royal livery without skimping. The royal livery was a distinctive uniform which showed that they were the king's servants, on all public occasions and on tour. This unique privilege made the new King's Men unassailable. They had the Globe, they were the first choice for court performances, and they had the incontestable power of the king's own name behind them.

As the King's Men, Shakespeare's company must have expected to make some kind of acknowledgement of their new patron in the plays they staged for him. When he came to England in 1603 he was famous for his mother, Mary Queen of Scots, whom Elizabeth had executed in 1586. He was also known for his books, including a handsomely printed book of advice to his son, *Basilikon Doron*. Shakespeare made some courteous and tactful

JAMES I

JAMES STUART was born in 1566, and was two years younger than Shakespeare. He became King James VI of Scotland when he was eighteen months old. His mother, Mary Queen of Scots, was forced to flee her throne and country leaving the young James behind. She was the daughter of James V, of Scotland and a niece of Henry VIII. James thus shared great-grandparents with Queen Elizabeth and was her closest surviving relative. Reassuringly for the English, who had lived for the last forty-four years under a childless queen, he had the right number of children, two sons and a daughter. He was a scholar and author, having written books about political theory, including *"The True Law"*, and a book, *Basilikon Doron*, ostensibly written as advice to his son and heir, which was obviously meant to be read by all as the definitive view of how monarchs should conduct themselves. He also wrote smaller things, such as a book about witchcraft, taking part in Scottish trials for witchcraft in the 1590s. All his books were re-issued in London in 1603.

This family tree *shows the relationship between Queen Elizabeth I (the Tudors) and James VI of Scotland (the Stuarts). The Stuarts were seen as the natural line of succession to the Tudor dynasty which had no direct heirs of its own. James VI of Scotland assumed the name of James I of England and VI of Scotland.*

● **Henry VII**
(King of England 1485-1509)
m. Elizabeth of York

Arthur
(d. 1502)
m. Catherine of Aragon

● **Henry VIII**
(King of England 1509-1547)

Margaret
m. ■ James V of Scotland
(King of Scotland 1509-1547)

Mary

■ **Mary Queen of Scots**
(Queen of Scotland 1547-1567)
m. Henry Stewart

married

Catherine of Aragon
(divorced 1533)

Anne Boleyn
(executed 1536)

Jane Seymour
(d. 1537)

Anne of Cleves
(divorced 1540)

Katherine Howard
(executed 1542)

Katherine Parr
(d. 1548)

● **Mary I**
(Queen of England 1553-1558)

● **Edward VI**
(King of England 1547-1553)

■ **James I of England (and VI of Scotland)**
(King of Scotland 1567-1625)
(King of England and Scotland 1603-1625)

● **Elizabeth I**
(Queen of England 1558-1603)

■ **Charles I**
(King of England 1625-1649)

● *Tudor Kings and Queens*
■ *Stuart Kings and Queens*

gestures towards the king's book in *Measure for Measure*, which was staged at court in 1604. But the flurry of plays that the new court demanded in their first two Christmas seasons was soon exhausted. The King's Men anxiously revived some of their old plays that the new Scottish courtiers had not seen, like *Love's Labours Lost*. But new plays were needed, and in 1605 Shakespeare turned back to his old source, Holinshed, for a story from Scottish history that related to James's own ancestors.

The result was *Macbeth*. This celebrated James's Scottish ancestry, which did not come down through Macbeth but through the true king Malcolm. It also picked up another interest of James, witchcraft. He had been angered by a book published in 1584, Reginald Scot's *Discoverie of Witchcraft*. Scot, a cool spirit who was sceptical of many of the more extravagant claims about witchcraft and demonology then current in England, had written an exposé of the magic tricks that alleged witches and wizards practised. Scot hated charlatans who played juggling tricks to

The witches *dominate the play of "Macbeth", enhancing the dark nightmare. They feed Macbeth's ambition with confusing prophecies, encouraging him to murder his king, Duncan. The dark evil of the witches tempt Macbeth to listen and believe he could have the throne of Scotland for himself. Below, Macbeth and Banquo confront the witches in the first act of the play.*

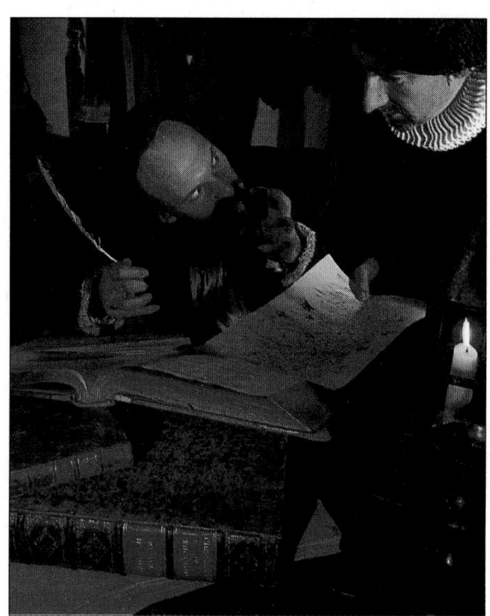

deceive innocent people, claiming that they were the work of God or the Devil. His book was widely read as much for its entertainment value as a record of different sorts of trickery and sleight of hand. The religious establishment at this time needed some sort of significant other, a Devil-figure who would convince everyone that evil was at large in the world. King James shared this conviction, and in 1597 he wrote a book about demons and evil spirits condemning Scot's views and claiming that witches really did exist.

Shakespeare picked up this feature of his patron's views to make a central element for *Macbeth*. *Faustus*, Christopher Marlowe's play about a man seduced by the devil, was a popular play on stage at this time. It was usually staged with spectacular effects, making devils run around the stage with fireworks spouting from their mouths and their breeches, and putting the fear of hell quite literally into the audience's minds. Edward Alleyn, who took the part of Faustus in its first famous years, always played him wearing a cross round his neck on stage as insurance, in case devils should really appear and try to drag him off to hell.

Shakespeare used some of *Faustus's* terrorising tactics for *Macbeth*. The three women, probably played by some of the men in the cast instead of the boys who usually took the women's parts, were called "black and midnight hags", but are not explicitly identified by name in the play as witches. Their spells, though, woven as they danced around their cauldron, are of the traditional kind that witches were said to use. Shakespeare even threw in a reference to a current story about a ship, the Tiger, which had been missing at sea off the coast of Africa for many months before it managed to return to London. The witches used the ordeal of the Tiger as a boast of what they could do. Their main function in the plot is to delude Macbeth with their prophecies, a complex process which opens out the self-deception in a man powerfully driven by ambition.

Playing the role of Faustus, Edward Alleyn had become the most famous player in London. Now he finally retired from acting to become an impresario and theatre manager. The King's Men continued to be led by the star player, Richard Burbage. He was everyone's hero, and the Globe audiences knew the quality they could expect. Burbage was so famous as Richard III that he was imitated in the streets. As one satirist put it: "Gallants, like Richard the usurper, swagger / That had his hand continual on his dagger."

Shakespeare could even play jokes with his audience about the actors. In *Hamlet* when young Hamlet is talking to Polonius about a visiting company of actors, Polonius says that he once played Julius Caesar in a play at university. Brutus killed me in the Capitol, he says, and Hamlet replies sarcastically, "It was a brute part of him to kill so capital a calf". The actor playing Polonius, probably John Heminges, had played Caesar only the year before, while Richard Burbage, now playing Hamlet, had played Brutus and killed Caesar-Heminges. That would be a good insider joke for everyone who remembered the other play. Then in the next scene, when Hamlet kills Polonius, the joke would suddenly turn doubly sour.

The intimacy that grew between audiences and actors, the familiarity of the star players and their closeness to those who came to the Globe was not just a matter of the players' ability to speak their soliloquies directly to the visible spectators. This intimacy between players

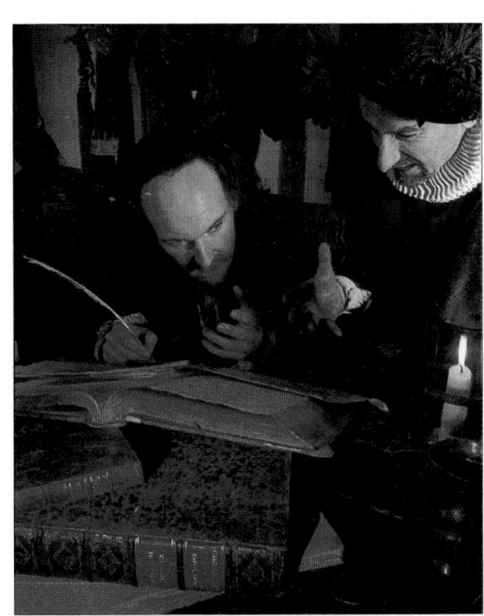

Shakespeare's writing *organised into comedies, histories, tragedies, poems and sonnets, printed and lined up on the shelf as modern books, rarely inspires us to reflect on the act of writing. He must often have been tired as he worked hard as an actor and shareholder, travelling and touring. There appear to have been years when he wrote two or more plays a year and then gaps when he may not have written at all. It is unlikely that he lived without ever suffering illness from the filth, poor diet and disease.*

and audience and the familiarity of the place and the occasion gave the first performances of Shakespeare's plays a richness that inevitably we have lost.

How long it took Shakespeare to write a play we cannot tell. The claim that *The Merry Wives of Windsor* took only three weeks may be true, especially since so much of it is in prose. Ben Jonson claimed to have written plays in six or seven weeks, and the payments from Philip Henslowe to his teams of writers suggest that they could usually produce a script in that amount of time. But Shakespeare's average rate of production during his twenty or so years in London was roughly two plays a year. He might have spent months or even years reading and considering subjects for his plays before he started composing the actual script. He was fairly distinctive for his time in writing alone, which suggests that he well knew how original and strong his personal work was. He may have contributed a few lines to *Sir Thomas More* in his early

years, and he helped the young John Fletcher to write two or three plays in his last years as a writer around 1612. He did not get drawn into the process of revising old plays, as Jonson did for a while. He knew what he could do, and he took his own time to do it.

The majority of Shakespeare's plays are written not in prose but in blank verse. Blank verse was first used by the Earl of Surrey in the time of Henry VIII for his translation of Virgil's *Aeneid*. Ever since Chaucer English verse

Reading out parts *in a new play was an important moment for the company. The players had discussed the story with Shakepeare already. He wrote parts with particular players in mind. It was the reaction of the company to their parts, that gave him the first opportunity to hear if the lines worked as he intended and whether the players were up to performing the roles he had given them.*

had been written in rhyme, in imitation of the French and Italian epic poets. There are fewer rhyming words in English than in Italian, but poets loyally followed the model. For his translation, Surrey kept the ten-syllable iambic pentameter, but on the grounds that Latin verse uses rhythm but not rhyme, he felt free to abandon rhyme for his verse. English rhythm of the time generally tried to imitate Latin. The term "iambic pentameter" is from the Latin, meaning a five-foot line with an iambic rhythm, each foot having one unstressed syllable followed by a stressed one. In fact Latin metre was based on long and short syllables, not stressed and unstressed. Strictly the English "iambic pentameter" is best defined as simply a ten-syllable line, with five of the ten syllables stressed, in a fairly regular sequence.

Surrey saw the strength of an unrhymed form, because it allowed the verse to flow more smoothly, without the pause and over-emphasis that the recurrent rhymes demand. It was called "blank" verse to distinguish it from the rhyming verse of Chaucer, which used the same metre for each line but rhymed each couplet or, in stanza forms, used cross-rhymes. It was this "blank" form that the playwrights seized on once they too decided to free themselves from rhyme. The length of the blank verse line, at ten syllables, suited the grammatical structure of English, the regular pause at each line-end creating a strong sentence structure and fitting the breathing pattern of the speaker.

Blank verse not only flowed more freely once released from the strait-jacket of rhyme, but it sounded more like normal speech. The first plays in this form deliberately used abnormal syntax, reversing the normal word-order and creating fresh emphasis, highlighting key words by putting them at line-ends. They also used much more colourful words than normal speech. So their verse was made to sound deliberately artificial. The strong rhythm was hypnotic. The speech flowed like music, with individual variations to emphasise key words or phrases. As time went on, even during the twenty years of Shakespeare's own writing career, blank verse gradually grew more like ordinary speech. His first plays, such as *Titus Andronicus*, and even *Romeo and Juliet*, are full of heavily artificial syntax and of words twisted into new meanings. In his later plays like *Coriolanus* and *The Tempest* it is often impossible to be sure when verse has not merged into prose. Editors usually print such speeches as verse, because they

***King Hamlet**, the ghost in the play of "Hamlet", is believed to have been played by William Shakespeare himself. Appearing from the trap door in the stage, the ghost confronts Hamlet and tells him he has been murdered by his brother, the new king, and wants revenge. The scene is set at midnight, but when the play was performed at the Globe, the ghost would have to convince the audience that he was an apparition of the night, in the daylight of an afternoon performance.*

CONDELL

HENRY CONDELL started playing as a hired man in Strange's company and after 1594 when the new companies were formed for London he joined the Chamberlain's Men as a hired man. He became a player sharer in the company in 1600 and worked steadily for the company until his death in 1626. Mostly he played secondary speaking parts, such as the Cardinal in Webster's *Duchess of Malfi* in 1614. By the 1620s he was giving up playing and taking on more and more of the company's management, including the editing of Shakespeare's plays for the First Folio of 1623.

LOWIN

JOHN LOWIN, a solid figure with a strong voice, joined the Chamberlain's Men in 1602, and worked for them for the next forty years. He became the King's Men's leading player along with Richard Burbage. He played major parts, and as a senior sharer and part-owner of the company's playhouses he took over the company's management once John Heminges finally retired in the late 1620s.

regard verse as superior to prose, and treat verse as the normal speech-pattern for the nobles in a play, whereas prose is used by clowns and commoners. But it is often not so easy to tell the one from the other.

The London playing companies went on tour for some part of the year in most years, out of habit as much as because the playhouses were closed because of the plague in the summer. Summer was in any case the best time of the year for travelling. In the country areas the mayors of towns often refused them permission to play if they were thought to come from plague-infested areas, and sometimes because they disapproved of plays altogether. In the later years, as the companies got more used to playing in London all the year round, they sent their junior players on tour, while the leading sharers stayed at home. Some of the senior player-sharers bought houses on what was then the outskirts of London, where they might shelter from the plague. By 1605 Shakespeare may have used these breaks for his visits to Stratford.

The King's Men did not travel as much as the lesser companies, but they did usually take part of the year on tour. They performed *Hamlet* in 1603 and *Volpone*, by Ben Jonson, in 1605 at Oxford and Cambridge, with both title roles played by Richard Burbage. In 1610 they performed *Othello* at Oxford. In a university town which had very divided views about the decadence of playgoing, they seem to have had a major triumph. There is an account (written in Latin) by a don in 1610 of how moving he found the play, particularly the face of the boy playing Desdemona when dead in bed. In translation it reads: "Not only by their speech but also by their deeds they drew tears. Indeed Desdemona, killed by her husband, although she always acted the matter very well, in her death moved us still more greatly; when lying in bed she implored the pity of those watching with her face alone."

The university authorities disapproved of professional playing, though not of students performing in their colleges to improve their public speaking skills. Like the Lord Mayor of London, and many of the mayors of the larger towns in England, the university authorities tried to stop the professional acting companies from playing at the university. When they were successful the players found that undergraduates travelled to taverns and inns outside the university control to see them perform.

The company's sharers settled into the specialised roles that suited their expertise. Richard Burbage, as promoter and financier to the company, might have been expected to take a more prominent role than he did in the company's direction. But he never wanted to be more than an actor, and became celebrated as London's

outstanding player. His fame made him accepted in a wide social circle. When he died in 1619 the Earl of Pembroke refused to see any plays for a while out of sorrow at the loss of the actor he called his "old acquaintance" Burbage. He was a painter in oils, probably composing the picture of himself that is in the collection at Dulwich Art Gallery near the College founded in 1619 by his stage rival Edward Alleyn.

The man who took care of the company's finances

Augustine Phillips *died before he had a chance to retire. A player of many parts, a musician, a writer of jigs, he left a lute, a bandore and a cittern, all stringed instruments, to his apprentices. His widow remarried unwisely and her new husband lost her shareholding in the Globe.*

The plague continued to close the London playhouses. The King's Men travelled with Richard Burbage as their star, visiting Oxford and Cambridge. William Shakespeare was thought to be with them some of the time.

was John Heminges. Widely respected and utterly trustworthy, he had a long experience in the theatre. He had been a fellow player with Tarlton in the Queen's Men in their great years, and later in Strange's Men at the Rose before the Chamberlain's Men were set up in 1594. Heminges was one of the very few financial directors who did not seek personal profit from his position, and financial loss and confusion occurred in almost every other playing company. He was inevitably appointed as a trustee in his fellow's wills to oversee and administer the dispersal of their money and possessions.

The company prospered tremendously in the years between the company becoming the King's Men in 1603 and the next long closure for plague in 1608-9. It took on some new actors as some of the old hands retired or died. Will Kemp left in 1599. George Bryan retired to become a groom at court by 1602. He was replaced by Henry Condell, a former hired man. John Lowin, who was to become one of the two leading players after Heminges and Condell retired, joined them in 1603. Augustine Phillips died in 1605. As each sharer left he or his widow were paid off and another man bought his way in. It was a close companionship, and few of them left with any signs of the animosity that seems to have accompanied Will Kemp's departure. In his will Augustine Phillips gave bequests to several of his fellow-players, including one to Laurence Fletcher, who had been wished on the company by King James. Fletcher had taken an English company to Scotland in the 1590s, and James remembered him when he came to England in 1603, naming him as one of the royal players. Phillips's bequests in his will are a striking example of the fellowship working together at the Globe.

THE GUNPOWDER PLOT

ENGLISH CATHOLICS had hoped that King James I, would show new tolerance towards them because of his Catholic wife, Queen Anne. However by April 1604 some Catholics were already plotting to kill him. In March 1605 they rented the crypt immediately beneath the Lords Chamber in the Houses of Parliament and there concealed thirty six barrels of gunpowder beneath firewood. Plague closed Parliament until 5th November. The delay raised doubts about sending 500 lords, some of them Catholics, to their deaths along with the Royal Family. One conspirator decided to warn his Catholic relation. The letter was shown to the king and the gunpowder was discovered at midnight on the 4th November along with Guy Fawkes, the man left to light the fuse. Eight of the conspirators survived capture to be beheaded in London, the other five were killed by their pursuers. As a result of the plot, Catholics were persecuted with even greater vigour.

The will was made on 4 May 1605, a little way out of London at Mortlake, where Phillips had recently bought a house and some land. One of his four daughters had married Robert Gough, who was in the company, and had been a boy player in the early 1590s. He witnessed the will. Beside the bequests to Phillips's immediate family, he gave a legacy of £5 to be distributed among the company's hired men, and thirty shillings each to Shakespeare, Henry Condell, and his former "servant", the player Christopher Beeston, who was now with Queen Anne's Men, the former Worcester's company. He gave twenty shillings each to Laurence Fletcher, the company clown Robert Armin, and to Richard Cowley, Alexander Cook and Nicholas Tooley, who had all been with Robert Gough in Strange's and the Chamberlain's. He gave silver bowls to the other leading sharers John Heminges, Richard Burbage and Will Sly. To the youths he had taught their acting trade he made special bequests of costumes, properties and musical instruments. To his "late apprentice" Samuel Gilburne he gave "my mouse-coloured velvet hose and a white taffeta doublet, a black taffeta suit, my purple cloak, my sword and dagger, and my bass viol". To James Sands, who was still "my apprentice" when Augustine Phillips died, he gave forty shillings and three stringed instruments " a cittern, a bandore and a lute". The clothing, the gentlemanly weapons and the musical instruments were all items for use in the profession of player.

Shakespeare had connections with the French Huguenots, a community of Protestants who were refugees from the religious wars that had been raging in France for the last thirty years. His Stratford friend Richard Field, who printed *Venus and Adonis* in 1593, had a Huguenot wife. She may have helped Shakespeare with the French spoken in *Henry V*. In 1599, now that his work was centred on the Globe in Southwark, Shakespeare moved into lodgings in the Liberty of the Clink, at the south

There was a large number *of popular songs to be heard on the streets of London. There were many skilled players from every section of society. Drums, pipes and viols produced loud music for jigs and country dances.*

end of London Bridge, where he paid his parish dues for the next few years. He seems not to have been so fond of the south bank, or of these lodgings, because by 1604, although still working at the Globe, he was back lodging in the northern suburbs where he started out. Conceivably he gave up his lodgings in the Clink to his young brother Edmund, who arrived to start a career as a player in London at about this time.

Shakespeare now went to live with a Huguenot family called Mountjoy. We know this because in a lawsuit of 1612 he was cited as a witness over a marriage settlement in 1604 concerning the Mountjoys' daughter. The 1612

***The Mountjoys** were famous for their quarrels and their wig making. Their, lodger William Shakespeare, is seen in his familiar role of promoting young love and living in the very midst of the sort of domestic comedy that he had so successfully used on stage in such plays as the "Merry Wives of Windsor".*

case was basically a lawsuit over how much the father had promised to pay in goods and money to the son-in-law as his daughter's dowry. Shakespeare's testimony was not very helpful. He said he could not remember any details. It may be that he preferred not to take sides, and was being tactful. The court found both men to be unsatisfactory and suggested a minimal settlement between them. In 1604 when Shakespeare found room in his house Christopher Mountjoy was a successful tire maker in Silver Street within the north west corner of the city walls. Tires were elaborate wigs, the grandest threaded with gold and silver and precious stones worn by the rich and by noble women including the Queen herself.

In 1604, the court King James established in London, following the plague, soon divided into three different parts. The official court of the king ran the central programme of events, including the ever-lengthening season of Christmas entertainments, which now ran from November right through to Shrove Tuesday, the beginning of the forty-day season of fasting before Easter. But the King hated London's crowds. His favourite pastime was hunting, and he usually spent as much time as he could chasing deer and keeping away from the court.

Somewhat out of the king's way, Queen Anne kept a court of her own at Somerset House. She had a close coterie of noble ladies. They patronised poets and writers, such as Samuel Daniel, who entertained them and dedicated their work to them. Quite early on, in late 1603, Anne took over the patronage of a company of boy players as well as her official adult group, appointing Daniel as their controller. They were clearly to be employed for her private entertainment. The French ambassador wrote home to Paris in 1604 about how scandalous it was that the Queen should be attending plays in which her husband was held up to ridicule while she enjoyed the laughs against her husband. The company she took on was the Blackfriars boys, who were running a

***The wigmaker's** raw materials included horse hair, and silk ribbons for wrapping around the wire that formed the frame, or tire, on which the elaborate structure of ladies' wigs depended.*

Richmond Palace *was set on the Thames some distance from London. It was thought to be more comfortable than the other royal palaces at the time. It was favoured by Prince Henry's court, for hunting and other sports.*

Princess Elizabeth *is seen here as a child. The only surviving daughter of James I and Queen Anne, in 1613 she married Prince Frederick, the Elector Palatine of the Rhine.*

repertoire of more and more scandalous and satirical plays. By 1608 they had caused so much trouble that the company was finally closed down altogether. That was when the Burbages at last retrieved the Blackfriars playhouse for their own company, The King's Men.

The third court, at Richmond, developed more slowly, because its focus, the young heir apparent, Prince Henry, was not old enough at first to have any control over his own affairs. Quite soon, though, discontent at James's preference for hunting over state business and his strong and consistent search for a foreign policy of peace rather than war, alienated many of his more aggressive and honour-seeking nobles. These nobles, and numbers of poets and writers seeking to make their way in the new world, started to draw together as a kind of alternative court around the young prince. George Chapman, a Henslowe playwright and a poet already famous for translating Homer into English, was one of these. Gradually this third court began to assert its own values and to mount its own shows. In the first Christmas seasons under James the prince had chiefly attended performances by the company that he patronised, Alleyn and Henslowe's Fortune playhouse group.

As Prince Henry grew older, his advisers began to move him in new directions. In a monarchy the education of the prince was a political matter of massive importance. *King Lear* was staged at court on Boxing Day 1606. Courtiers would have noted the story of the Dukes of Albany and Cornwall, which were the titles of King James' two sons, and the aptness of a play about "the division of the Kingdoms". That issue was then before Parliament, which was resisting the King's idea of uniting his two kingdoms of England and Scotland. What the effect on the young princes might have been we cannot say. Henry died in 1612 when he was fifteen. Shakespeare appears to have taken no direct part in this attempt to influence England's future by shaping the mind of the child who everyone expected would be its next king. He never worked under the court's direction.

The original version of *King Lear* was recorded in a rather odd text printed in a quarto in 1608. A rather different text appeared in the First Folio in 1623. It is possible that the later Folio text may have been revised for a new production in 1611, when line 3 of the play, which referred to "the division of the kingdoms" in the quarto text, was changed to "the division of the kingdom". This change, small as it is, may have become appropriate once the union of the two kingdoms of England and Scotland, a hot subject of debate between the king and his parliament in 1605, had been rejected by parliament.

One of the features of both texts for *King Lear* is the stage directions for the storm scene in Act III. Modern actors often have difficulty making themselves heard over the noise of the storm, and they sometimes insist on muted effects or an intermittent series of noises that gives the actor time to speak his lines before the backstage effects drown them again. In Shakespeare's texts the stage directions say "storm still", while Lear is roaring at the tempest. Sound effects for storms were produced by two devices: either a large bullet was rolled down a chute made of lead to make a long-drawn-out rumbling noise, or drums were used for the louder cracks of thunder. Ben Jonson, typically scornful of such attempts at stage realism, wrote in a Folio edition of his own plays published in 1616 in the preface to *Every Man In his Humour* of how mercifully free his play was from the effects of the "rolled bullet heard / To say, it thunders; nor tempestuous drum / Rumbles, to tell you when the storm doth come". It has been suggested that Shakespeare took the part of the Earl of Gloucester in *King Lear*. If so, he would have experienced the problem of the players competing with these offstage sound effects at first hand.

PRINCE HENRY

PRINCE HENRY was the eldest son of King James I. Even as a young boy he enjoyed public displays of princely power. He favoured war and confrontation with England's traditional enemies, unlike his father, who was intent on making peace with Spain. A court of convinced Protestant warriors gathered round the Prince promoting leadership, horsemanship, arts and science. Henry was to be their ideal king. He died when he was just eighteen in 1612. His brother Prince Charles became King of England and Scotland in 1625.

***Queen Anne** was the daughter of the King of Denmark, and her brother became King Christian IV of Denmark. She married King James when he was King of Scotland. Her son, Prince Charles, became King Charles I of England. In London she had her own court, her own company of players and she performed herself in masques.*

William Shakespeare's own attitudes in politics and life are elusive apart from the personal revelations in the sonnets. We have to judge what most interested him from the subjects he chose to write about, and from the changes he introduced to his source-texts. That he was supremely humane and supremely sensitive to every kind of personality and every human obsession, is self-evident. What his personal prejudice and his personal opinions may have been is more difficult to discover.

His portrait of the Jew in *The Merchant of Venice* is warmer than Marlowe's portrait of a Jew is in *The Jew of Malta*. Shakespeare, however, still satisfied the prejudice of his time by forcing Shylock, the Jew of Venice, to convert to Christianity at the end of the play. His portrait of the Moor in *Othello* shows a marked difference from the common prejudices. He reversed the usual stereotypes of his day, making the dark skinned Moor a great general and transferring the character of evil and dark murderer to the white Venetian who looks like a simple soldier. Shakespeare was always on the side of the young in marriage. His plays invariably favour young lovers over the parents who assert their traditional right to choose who their children will marry. This made his attitude distinctly radical, when marriage was chiefly concerned with financial settlements and the ownership of property. A wife's identity was described in terms of money, goods and land.

Shakespeare's politics are even more elusive, despite the fact that all of his serious plays, from *Titus Andronicus* in the early 1590s to *The Tempest*, first per-

***"King Lear"** was performed by the King's Men for the Christmas revels of 1606. There are references to uniting kingdoms and other political topics of the day. It is a play in which King Lear's mad ravings against ingratitude may have been sympathetic to James I who had survived the Gunpowder plot the previous November. The small princes may have seen William Shakespeare performing in the role of Earl of Gloucester, who is blinded in the play.*

formed in 1610, were intimately concerned with political principles and practices. *Titus Andronicus* opens with the Romans confronting a choice between the three standard ways of choosing a ruler. Their eventual choice, the dead emperor's eldest son, was the normal practice in choosing the kings of England. In Titus' Rome it leads to murder, rape, and cannibalism. *The Tempest* uses young love, carefully stage-managed by an exiled duke, to

Plays 1601 - 1609

Even if he had written nothing else, *Hamlet* would have immortalised William Shakespeare. Its fame was immediate, and its hero has never ceased to fascinate readers and audiences in every century and every country of the world. It took his own writing in a fresh direction too. After *Twelfth Night* had wound up the "What You Will" series of light comedies, he wrote two more complex and less directly funny comedies, *All's Well that Ends Well* and *Measure for Measure*, and then gave up writing light hearted plays altogether until 1607, when *Pericles* appeared. Instead he wrote the great tragedies, *Othello, King Lear, Timon of Athens* and *Macbeth*. When he turned back to romantic comedy with *Pericles* he also turned back to the series set in Roman history that he had abandoned in 1599. In 1607 and 1608 he wrote *Antony and Cleopatra* and *Coriolanus*, each of them an amazingly subtle analysis of quite different political issues. The first concluded the story launched with *Julius Caesar*, presenting the intricate power games played between the rival contenders for the imperial crown of Rome. The second was set in the earliest days of the Roman republic, before its rise to greatness, and shows the conflict between the city's patrician nobles, who think they own the city, and the plebeian workers who believe in the civic 'liberties' which led them to expel Rome's former kings. The company had, at that time, one superb boy actor, who played Cleopatra in the first play and Coriolanus' mother Volumnia in the second.

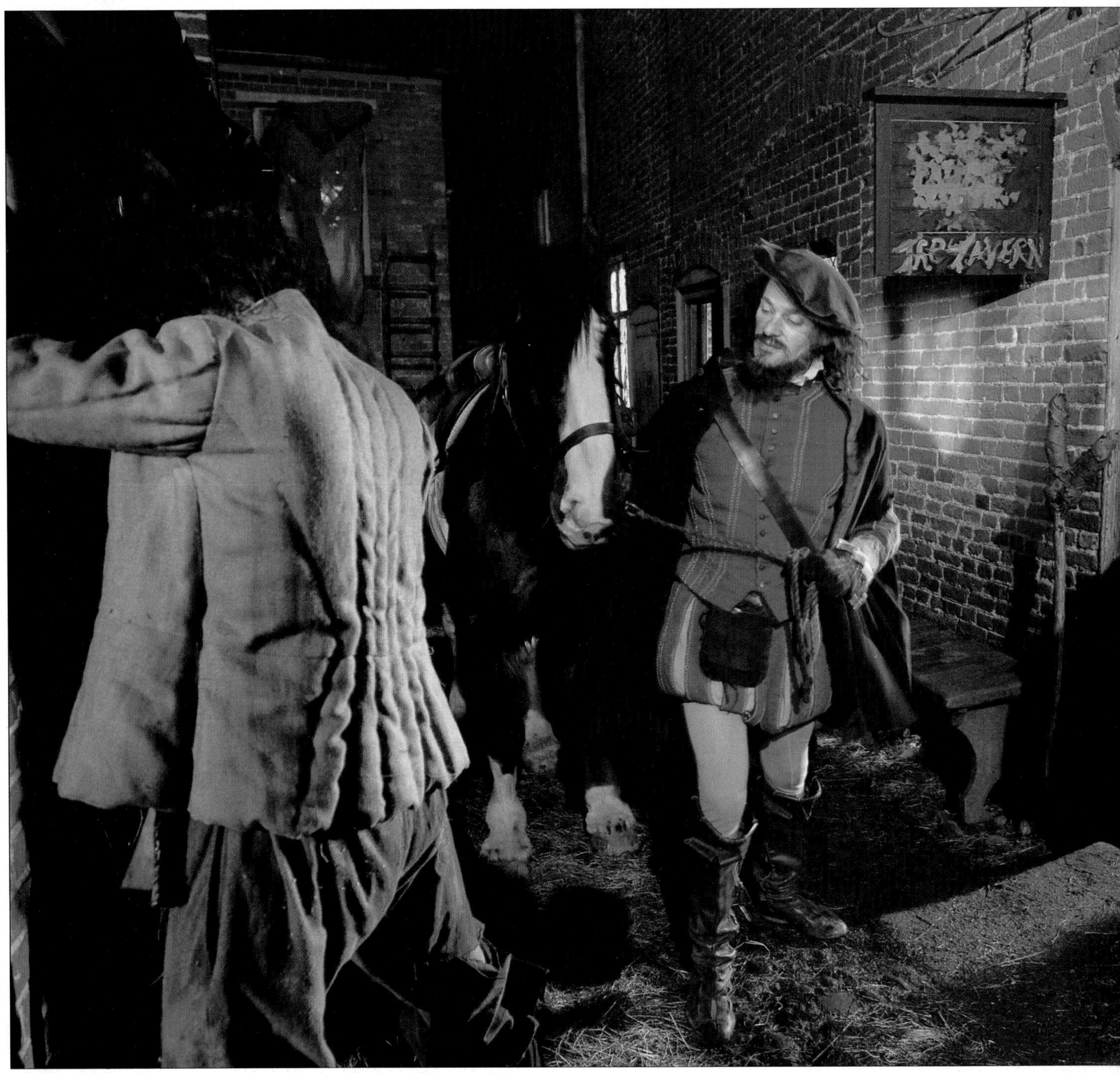

restore him to his dukedom and make his heirs rulers of the kingdom to which his dukedom had been made subject. Shakespeare's portrait of the greatest hero-king from England's own history, Henry V, does not flinch from showing him as cold and ruthless, ordering the French prisoners at Agincourt to be slaughtered to ensure his victory. To the humane, politics is ugly, and its seamier sides are displayed throughout Shakespeare's plays based on English and Roman history.

For all the little hints about rivalry between the leading companies the years following the succession of King James I were a good and prosperous time for both of them. They both had new playhouses, one the Globe in Southwark and the other the Fortune in Clerkenwell. Other companies, including the boy groups at St. Paul's and the Blackfriars theatre, contended with them for a place in London, but the King's Men had the favour of the Master of the Revels as well as the Privy Council, and they also had the most popular plays in town. It had taken the Admiral's Men longer to be established as the Prince's Men, serving the heir apparent Prince Henry. In 1603 Will Kemp led a company which was allocated to Queen Anne,

though they came out much more slowly than plays had done in the years of his highest rate of production through the 1590s. Then in about 1607 his writing changed again, and his rate of production redoubled. He started not only a run of "romances", the great and wholly new style of tragicomedies including *Cymbeline, The Winter's Tale* and *The Tempest*, of which *Pericles* was the first, but he also renewed the sequence of Roman plays which he had abandoned after *Julius Caesar* in 1599. *Antony and Cleopatra* and *Coriolanus* were a less drastic new start than the tragicomedies, but they are still distinct from the great tragedies in that they focus on personalities rather than moral issues. Through the four years from 1607 to 1610 he produced nearly two plays a year.

During all these years Shakespeare continued to act with the company. He is on record as playing in Jonson's tragedy *Sejanus*, though we do not know which role he took in his own plays. These were the years in which he most probably was allocated the "kingly parts" that John Davies of Hereford hailed him for in 1610.

All his working life *William lived in lodgings in London and sent money back to Stratford. He did not buy his own place in London until he had returned to live almost full time in Stratford. His investments in Stratford in property and business make it clear that his plan was always to return there and, whatever had passed in London, take up life with Anne again.*

The most comfortable way *to travel back to Stratford was to ride, stopping along the road at Oxford. Many rumours were circulated in later years that William fathered a child with the beautiful wife of a tavern keeper Mistress Davenant. He was known to stop at the tavern but may have passed the night innocently next door at the Cross Inn.*

who also gave her name to the Blackfriars boys. The King's Men were pre-eminent, but all three of the adult companies had royal protection and could wear the scarlet royal livery.

Although these were the King's Men's great years, for reasons we can only speculate over, Shakespeare's rate of play production in this period began to slow down quite markedly. He wrote fewer comedies, probably composing none at all between *Measure for Measure* in 1603 and *Pericles* in 1607. He concentrated instead on writing the great tragedies, *Othello, King Lear* and *Macbeth*, even

CHAPTER SEVEN

SUCCESS AND DISASTER

ALL THREE COMPANIES of players, the King's, Queen's and Prince's Men, and the one surviving company of boy players at the Blackfriars theatre, did well until the plague returned in 1608. The virulence of the plague brought a long closure, from the spring of 1608 through the whole of 1609. The King's Men could survive it; indeed they were given another grant by the king to help keep them going through the closure. But the other companies were more precariously placed. The boy company, already in serious trouble with the King and the Master of the Revels for the satirical and critical content of their plays, did not survive. In August 1608 the boy company's manager, as the lessee of their Blackfriars playhouse, closed the company down and surrendered his lease to the Burbages. Now at long last the Burbages had their inheritance. It meant that when playing resumed after the plague epidemic they could finally open at the hall playhouse in the most desirable section of the city, just as had been planned thirteen years before by their father, James Burbage.

The difference for the Burbages in 1608 to those unhappy days in 1596, was that they had the Globe. Now what they chose to do was oddly quixotic, and certainly unprofitable to them as business men. Having lived for nine years with the success of the arrangement at the Globe, where the leading player-sharers also co-owned their theatre as housekeepers, they opted to extend the Globe idea to the Blackfriars. The two Burbage brothers sold some of their freehold in the Blackfriars playhouse to a consortium consisting very largely of the same people who were already housekeeper sharers in the Globe.

The Blackfriars benefited in having as part of its assets, permanent musicians, at a time when music was almost a second language, played, sung and understood at all levels of society.

The Blackfriars Boys were closed down because of their performances which mocked the moral order and satirised the Scottish court. By 1608, they could hardly be described as boys. The star, Nathan Field, a former pupil at St.Paul's school, was twenty one years old and writing plays. All the boys were experts on playing indoors where theatrical make-up and costume were lighted mainly by candles.

They brought in one financier from outside, but otherwise all the sharers in the new playhouse were sharers in the King's Men. Thus the same consortium, chiefly the leading players, held controlling shares in the Blackfriars and the Globe. From here on Shakespeare, with his partners, began to make a lot of money from the rent of both premier playhouses in London.

For the first time one company now had two playhouses. Instead of using just one of the playhouses themselves and renting the other out to another company, they chose to use both, and to keep one of them empty through half the year. They played at the open-air Globe through the summer months and the Blackfriars through the winter. King James had by now created new companies for each of his children, so there was a surplus of licensed companies and a shortage of licensed playhouses. So the King's Men could have been sure of collecting rent. However, they had grown to like the Globe, and did not wish to abandon it for the Blackfriars.

Many benefits and some constraints came with this new playhouse. Along with the theatre, for instance, the company acquired the famous Blackfriars consort of musicians. Consorts, usually comprising woodwinds and stringed instruments, never brass, could only play indoors. In the open-air playhouses, the Globe's central balcony room was altered to make a curtained off music room. Along with such a genteel acquisition came the much richer clientele of the Blackfriars. The new venue had an audience of gentry and ladies, who preferred attending the hall playhouses rather than the open playhouses like the Globe which attracted the whole range of London's population. This tradition was easily maintained at the Blackfriars, because it charged a minimum of six times the Globe's cheapest entry price. It did however, have some drawbacks for the players. Its stage was half the size of the Globe's, and its acting space was reduced even further by the dozen or more gallants who paid for stools to sit on the stage itself to watch the plays.

***Shakespeare wrote** his play "The Tempest" for the Blackfriars playhouse. It was a play written to tease the audience, where nothing is ever what it seems. The survivors from the opening scene of shipwreck were instructed to appear in wet clothes to make their escape from drowning realistic. Otherwise the stage used only the most basic scenery to suggest the island-setting of the play. However, music was very important to emphasise the magic power of Prospero, the hero and magician of "The Tempest".*

Prince Charles *was the younger son of King James I. His elder brother Henry had been promoted as the ideal prince. Chivalrous, honourable and upholder of the Protestant faith, he was educated to be anointed King. The death of Prince Henry in 1612 thrust Prince Charles, aged twelve, into that same role but without the previous ten years of grooming. He did not have his elder brother's aesthetic interests or his athletic prowess. He became King Charles I in 1625. He was executed in 1649 by order of Parliament.*

Shakespeare wrote only one of his plays specifically for the new indoor theatre. He did so daringly, with his tongue in his cheek. The Blackfriars audience expected to be lulled, before the play, by an hour or so of sophisticated music from the Blackfriars consort. English music by Tallis, Byrd, Morley and others was famous throughout Europe at this time. Much of it was written to be sung by secular voices as well as music composed for the church. It was believed that earthly music was an imperfect echo of the heavenly music of the spheres, or planets and its harmonies were thought to bring reassurance about human mastery over chaos.

The Tempest began as soon as the orchestra had completed its soothing overture,with a stunningly loud storm designed deliberately to startle. On stage a ship is caught in the storm and strikes the rocks of a foreign coast, its crew and its royal passengers helpless against the forces of nature. The audience is then told that it had all been merely a design of the magician Prospero's art, and that nobody had been hurt by it. The play was as neatly calculated to confront the audiences at the Blackfriars as was Ben Jonson's companion-play, *The Alchemist*, also about the workings of a magician.

The Tempest shows other signs of the company's move to the Blackfriars. Apart from offstage music, a series of songs was written for the spirit Ariel to sing. It required more elaborate staging than the Globe plays, including some spectacular costume changes and special effects. A banquet was set out for the King of Naples and his courtiers on a table. While the audience stared at the apparition of a winged harpy, the table-top was spun upside down, leaving bare wood, so that it appeared to the audience that, as the play's stage direction puts it, "with a quaint device the banquet vanishes". The finale was marked by a "discovery scene", in which the King of Naples finds that his son has not been drowned in the opening tempest but is alive and moreover that he has a lover. In this moment of "discovery" the young lovers, Prospero's daughter Miranda and Ferdinand, the king's son, are revealed playing together when the stage hangings are drawn back. What they are doing though is not quite as might be expected. They are obeying Prospero's injunction to be virtuous by playing chess. Shakespeare took his brilliant art lightly by this point in his career.

1610 was the year in which Prince Henry was invested as the heir to James I with the title of Prince of Wales. It was gloriously stage managed by the Prince's faction with a mixture of masque and tournament. So, in a tournament attack the Prince and his few supporters as men of

Late plays

After writing *Macbeth* in 1606, Shakespeare's rate of play writing increased. He returned to the Roman Histories with *Coriolanus* and *Antony and Cleopatra*, and launched a new kind of play with *Pericles*. It is variously called a 'romance', or a 'tragicomedy' or more neutrally a 'late play'. *Pericles* was followed in the years up to 1610 by *Cymbeline, The Winter's Tale* and *The Tempest*. Each of these plays is a sophisticated game of play-making, using and misusing the old conventions with incredible skill and ease. The old tricks such as jealous kings, mistaken identity, long lost children, and deadly poisons are redeployed in a deliberately non-serious way. The king's errors are safely corrected, the long lost children are found and all the poisons turn out to be sleeping potions.

The Tempest is sometimes seen as Shakespeare's farewell to his profession, since its leading character, Prospero, is a magician who controls the stage illusions throughout the play (even including occasional bouts of bad temper when he forgets his own plots), and who at the end bids farewell to his 'art' in the epilogue. This is one of the less likely readings of Shakespeare's plays as autobiography, since, although he had retired to Stratford when he wrote it, he did go on writing plays in the same tragi-comic and romantic form, in collaboration with the younger writer John Fletcher, who joined the company as a poet or playwright, in 1609. They shared the writing of at least three plays, *The Two Noble Kinsmen*, the lost play *Cardenio*, staged at court in 1613 and *Henry VIII*, when one of the more pretentious features of its staging, a cannon-shot, succeeded in burning the Globe playhouse to the ground.

"chivalry and honour" defended themselves successfully against overwhelming numbers. Meanwhile, the sale of knighthoods to those with sufficient money was open and the King's first minister, Robert Cecil, tried to clear the King's debts of over £600,000 with parliament. There was a sense of fantasy triumphing over reality in government.

Masques cost as much as £3000 to stage, and even the most modest masque cost a lot. Ben Jonson was paid £20 for writing a masque for Robert Cecil in 1607. The famous player Edward Alleyn was tempted out of retirement to appear in it for a further £20. The designer Inigo Jones also received £20. The rest of the money was spent on scenery and effects which might include wafted perfumes, clouds of rose petals, mock hunts; there was little to constrain the imagination in the creative hands of Inigo Jones. Ben Jonson inevitably fell out in his successful and lucrative collaboration with Jones, and equally inevitably had the last vengeful word, "Oh, to make boards to speak! There is the task / Paint and carpentry are the soul of masque". William Shakespeare took no part in the masque making business. *The Tempest* has part of one in its fourth Act, but it is broken off before it can be completely shown.

The time between the shock given to the first Blackfriars audiences by *The Tempest* and its selection for presentation at court was the usual one. The Master of the Revels made sure that the plays he chose for the court performances were already clear successes before he would take them up for the royal pleasure through the long Christmas season. *The Tempest* opened the season at court on 1 November 1611 and *The Winter's Tale* followed it on 5 November. As the Company's two latest hits, Shakespeare's plays were the main feature of the King's Mens repertoire, both at court and in London.

In the 1612-13 season at court there were seven Shakespeare plays, some performed twice, plus three by Beaumont and Fletcher, the rising new team of King's Men's writers, and six by other playwrights, including

***William Shakespeare** and John Fletcher meet at a London "ordinary" to discuss writing together a new history play, "Henry VIII". The play relied on showing King Henry, in pageant and procession, heralded by cannon fire. The third performance at the Globe set the playhouse on fire.*

***Overleaf** The Globe ablaze. An onlooker described the moment when the audience 'thought at first but an idle smoke, and their eyes more attentive to the show, it kindled inwardly, and ran round like a train, consuming within less than an hour, the whole house to the very grounds'.*

Jonson's *Alchemist*. For the next thirty years a majority of the plays that the King's Men's offered at court were old favourites by Shakespeare. In January 1613, the wedding, postponed because of Prince Henry's death, between his sister Princess Elizabeth and the Elector Palatine took place with fourteen plays by the King's Men. The company received £153.6s.8d for their work. It was after this that William made his first known purchase of any property in London. He bought an apartment in the Blackfriars gatehouse as did Richard Burbage. It suggests that he intended to continue visiting London well into the future. It was conveniently close the Blackfriars playhouse.

Through his last years William was not cut off from the associations which had been so profitable to him in his twenty years in London. *The Tempest*, although written late in 1610 and therefore very likely from his Stratford home, shows evidence of his concerns for the correct staging of his plays. He assigned twenty-five lines to be spoken on stage, so the spirit, Ariel, had time to make a costume change between appearances. A few more lines had to be allowed for changing into the Harpy costume. It suggests that he was working on the basis of practical tests about how long it would take the boy playing Ariel to change. There was also his writing in collaboration with John Fletcher when Fletcher's long standing partner Francis Beaumont left for Leicestershire and a wealthy marriage.

It was, of course, a play written with Fletcher, *Henry VIII*, which required a cannon-shot that set the Globe's thatched roof alight and burned it down to its foundations. According to the accounts of the disaster nobody was killed, although one account says that a man's trousers caught fire and were quenched with a bottle of ale. Another account of the fire said that although "the house was very full" everyone escaped "all without hurt except one man who was scalded with the fire by adventuring in to save a child which otherwise had been burned". This account of a heroic act does not mention the convenient bottle of ale. Whatever the heroics, the loss of the Globe set the company and its landlords the senior sharers, including Shakespeare, a major problem.

The company still had the Blackfriars as an alternative playhouse, and they could have left the Globe's remains untouched, and given up the lease. Instead they chose to dig into their pockets, and paid out a huge sum to rebuild it more lavishly than before. This is the time when Shakespeare may have left the company and sold his shares in the two theatres, so we do not know whether he helped to pay for the second Globe. His will seems to indicate that some time before he died he had given up his shares in the Globe and the Blackfriars theatres, and also his rooms in the Blackfriars gatehouse. If so, the burning of the Globe may have marked his final withdrawal from the city which had seen his greatest triumphs.

By 1613 it is likely that life in London had become a much less attractive proposition to an ageing poet than it had been to the younger man in the 1590s. Now, under the Stuarts, life for the poets and playwrights was becoming increasingly a struggle for preferment at court. Those lucky few who were chosen to write masques, such as Jonson, Chapman, Daniel and later Middleton, were the

***The King's Men** had to save their greatest treasures, the book box, containing the parts and prompt copies of the plays they owned, and their costumes. The costumes for "Henry VIII" were very elaborate and enormously expensive, costing far more than the plays.*

***The Globe burnt**, like so many Tudor buildings, without warning and very quickly on 29th June 1613. The King's Men, the most stable, and united company, rebuilt it in 1614 at a cost of £1,400. This was an enormous sum of money to pay out for a playhouse used for only the five summer months of each year.*

ones who could consider themselves a cut above the scribblers of the Henslowe stable.

Ben Jonson still wrote for the popular stage, but his eye was now increasingly on his noble patrons and the masques which the court saw as his greatest achievements. In many ways his career is a perfect contrast to that of Shakespeare. Both of them started from poor origins as stage-players, and rose to eminence by their writing for the stage. After his early start with his Ovid-based poems dedicated to the Earl of Southampton Shakespeare avoided noble patrons. From 1594 onwards he never wrote for any employer beside his acting company. Jonson, by contrast, sold his work widely, not just to the players but to the court and to a range of noble patrons, for whom he wrote many poems. After the publication of the Folio edition of his best plays in 1616 he stopped writing for the stage altogether for nearly ten years, instead writing poems and lecturing on rhetoric to

__Ben Jonson__, Richard Burbage, old rivals and old friends, meet up with Shakespeare on one of his rare visits to London.

the gentry of Gresham's College, a group of scholars in London. The Earl of Pembroke secured him a Master of Arts degree from Oxford. King James gave him a pension. By the 1620s copies of the Folio of his plays were in the personal library of every well-read young gentleman.

Ambitious poets, starting with Beaumont and Fletcher, who exchanged their play manuscripts with Jonson and wrote commendatory verses for their publication, had always gathered round him, calling themselves the "Sons of Ben". His career as a poet was finally rewarded, when he was made in practice, if not in direct financial reward, the first poet laureate, official court poet to King Charles I late in the 1630s. He was massively overweight and self-indulgent in his personal habits and was finally crippled by a stroke. For all the devotion of the "Sons of Ben", his last years were miserably painful and poverty-stricken in contrast to Shakespeare's comfortable retirement in Stratford.

CHAPTER EIGHT

COUNTRY GENTLEMAN

By 1613 most of Shakespeare's time was taken up by his business affairs in Stratford. The evidence of his activities in Stratford from 1609 on indicates that he had made up his mind to settle and concentrate on running his Stratford house and lands. He would continue writing for the King's Men but only make occasional excursions back to London. He did a lot of tidying up in 1609, including calling in old debts from his father's time. He knew what he was doing. The records show that he had been planning it ever since he started sending money back home from London in the 1590s.

It was a comfortable new life, though not without its turmoils. A fire burned more than fifty houses, stables and barns in Stratford on 9 July 1614, though none of the Shakespeare properties was damaged. The community made calls on his services as a major property owner and a possible benefactor to the town. Taking care of all his diverse investments took time and there were fewer members of the family to help him. His most business-minded brother, Gilbert, had died in 1612, and his last brother, Richard, died in 1613. This left only himself and his sister Joan Hart from the substantial family of John and Mary Shakespeare still alive. Joan lived in the family house in Henley street that belonged to her brother.

Shakespeare's own daughter Susanna was more literate than most of her peers in Stratford and could sign her name. She had made a good marriage in 1607, when she was aged twenty five, but her younger sister Judith was still unmarried in 1615 when she was thirty, and must have been a worry to her parents. Susanna had married a Cambridge graduate, a physician named John Hall, a sensitive and capable man. Their heir, a daughter named Elizabeth, was born in 1608. They continued to live in the Shakespeare properties in Stratford until the line died out with Elizabeth in 1670.

Some of John Hall's writings survive. His job as a country doctor locked him into the worst of Warwickshire's life and death. Shakespeare in *Troilus and Cressida* described the familiar ailments as "the rotten diseases of the south, the guts-griping, ruptures,

***William Shakespeare** and his granddaughter Elizabeth play together at New Place in Stratford. William enjoyed his retirement from London as a leading citizen in Stratford. His wealth protected him and his wife Anne from bad harvests and inflation that devastated the rural poor.*

***William Shakespeare** at home with his family. Back row: William; his son-in-law, Dr.John Hall; his younger daughter, Judith Shakespeare. Middle row: Anne Shakespeare; his married daughter, Susanna Hall; Judith's fiancé, Thomas Quiney. In front: his grand-daughter Elizabeth who was to be the only surviving member of this family and died without any heirs.*

catarrhs, loads o' gravel i'the back, lethargies, cold palsies, raw eyes, dirt-rotten livers, wheezing lungs, bladders full of impostume, sciatics, lime-kilns in the palm, incurable bone-ache, and the rivelled fee-simple of the tetter". His standard cures, as noted in his records, were generally more moderate than some in that time.

Judith's career was more eventful and less harmonious than her sister's. She married one of the sons of an old family friend, Adrian Quiney, a Stratford wine seller, on 10 February 1616, when she was thirty-one. The wedding took place during Lent when marriages were normally prohibited. Her husband, Thomas Quiney, was already in trouble. He had made another woman pregnant, and in March, a month after the wedding, she died in childbirth along with her child. Thomas was excommunicated for his untimely wedding and tried for fornication in the Stratford ecclesiastical court, though he got off fairly lightly with a fine. It was not an auspicious start to Judith's married life.

Less than a month before he died Shakespeare adjusted his provisions for Judith in his will. The first version was drawn up in January, by the lawyer he had used for the last decade, Francis Collins. He came back on 25 March to make changes as a result of Judith's marriage. Shakespeare was evidently in a sickly condition for much of that winter, and the fact that he made his will indicates that he thought he would soon die. His signatures on the three pages of the revised will made at the end of March show signs of physical weakness. It is, however, just possible that he did not follow the usual practice and make his will only when he thought he was dying, but did so because of Judith's marriage. The fact that he made both versions of the will in the last four months of his life, though, does suggest that he knew he was dying and he may well have been suffering from a long illness.

Judith's marriage was evidently expected when the first version of the will was made in January. It included a provision for the newly-wedded pair as its first concern. But the public scandal of Thomas Quiney's fornication made Shakespeare call for changes to be made to protect Judith against a man whom her father seems not to have trusted. Thomas Quiney's subsequent standing in Stratford and his behaviour as a citizen seems to give some backing to that judgement. He became a burgess on the council and later the chamberlain, but he was never elected to the status of alderman.

In the revised version of Shakespeare's will, the original bequest of £100 to his son-in-law as a dowry went instead directly to Judith as her marriage portion. He gave her a further £50 in return for her renouncing any claim to a cottage in Chapel Lane which backed on to New Place. Among his personal bequests he gave Judith a "broad silver-gilt bowl".

In the event Judith lived on until she was seventy-seven, outliving her father by nearly forty-six years and her husband by at least fifteen. She had three children, all boys, but one died while still a baby and the other two in 1639, aged nineteen and twenty-one. When Susanna's daughter Elizabeth died the Shakespeare line died out.

Shakespeare's sister Joan was left £20 and his clothes, and her three sons £5 each. His grand-daughter, Susanna's child, inherited all the family plate apart from the bowl for Judith. Susanna and her husband had New Place. The rest of the will gave bequests to the poor of Stratford and to a few friends, and the "second-best bed" to his wife. The possible ironies in this have been much-debated, but it was the marriage bed (the best one was for important guests). For her other needs Anne would be provided for by her daughter Susanna, with whom she continued to live at New Place. The Londoners, Burbage, Heminges and Condell received each 26s 8d (two marks, a little over £1) to buy memorial rings.

In his will, the only record of his London years is the bequests he left to his former fellows. It is possible that he still had his shares in the two playhouses, but if so they did not come in for any special note. They would have gone with the rest of his property, his father's rambling house in Henley Street, the big house called New Place, and all the Warwickshire lands that he had acquired over the last twenty years, to the Halls. Since there is no mention of a Hall share in the legal documents written over a dispute about renewing the Globe's lease in 1635 it seems unlikely that the Halls kept any interest in the London theatres. The only London property mentioned in the will was the Blackfriars gatehouse, which also went to Susanna. In the absence of any note like the one for the Blackfriars holding which had probably been rented out,

__The final will__ of Shakespeare was feebly signed and it has been assumed that he was aware that he was close to death. The will does not mention either his books, or any copies he may have kept of his plays. The Bodleian library in Oxford, created at this time, took the decision that playscripts were unworthy to be included amongst the books in their collection. It is possible that Susanna and her husband, John Hall, were the literate members of the family and therefore kept and eventually lost William's books.

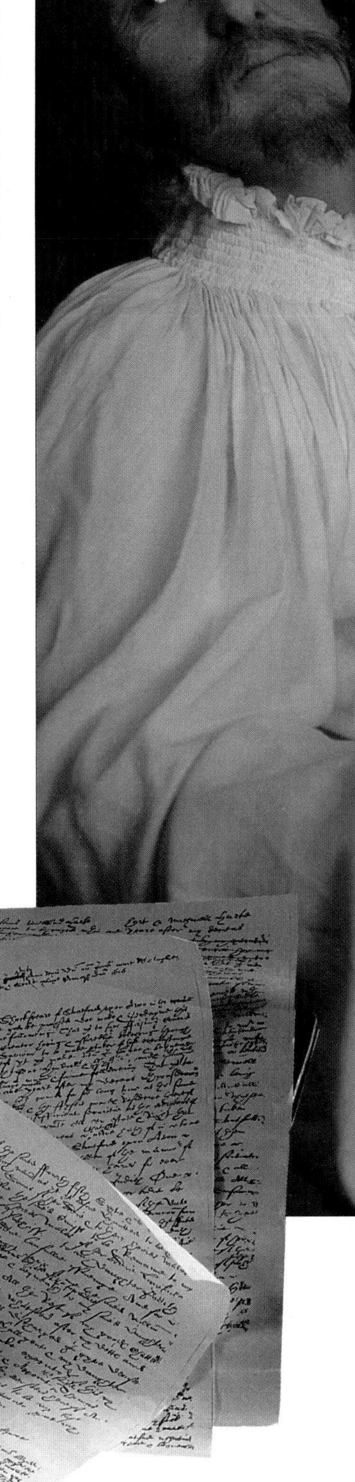

it appears that he had already disposed of the playhouse shares to his fellows in London. There is no mention of any special concern for his books and papers.

Shakespeare died at home in Stratford on 23 April 1616, almost the same day as his birth. He was survived by his wife, who lived until 1623, and his two daughters. After his death the stonemason Gheerart Janssen, whose workplace was in Southwark near the Globe, made a bust of him. Originally painted in lifelike colours, it still stands on his tomb in the parish church of Holy Trinity at Stratford. A few years later an engraving was made by Martin Droeshout, a twenty-two-year-old Londoner of Flemish descent, for the First Folio. Droeshout was probably too young to have seen Shakespeare in the flesh. Whether Janssen remembered him from his Globe days we do not know. His is the more conventional portrayal, a bland kind of memorial bust of the sort which usually offered only a fairly general resemblance to the original. But Droeshout's is the more immature work of the two, and not informed by any personal familiarity with the subject. Still, Jonson praised the engraving's likeness to Shakespeare, in a verse published with it in the Folio. Those two representations are all there is to show Shakespeare's real face.

***Dr. John Hall** attended Shakespeare in his last illness. Doctoring had more in common with magic than medicine, with potions of spider web, flowers, herbs and cures involving purges and bleedings. A solicitor and friend, Francis Collins, waits for William to find the strength to sign his will. The enormous quantity of legal documents provide the detail of William Shakespeare's life.*

***Overleaf** William Shakespeare is dead and laid out, pennies close his eyes. He was the first Shakespeare to be given the privilege of a marked grave inside the church.*

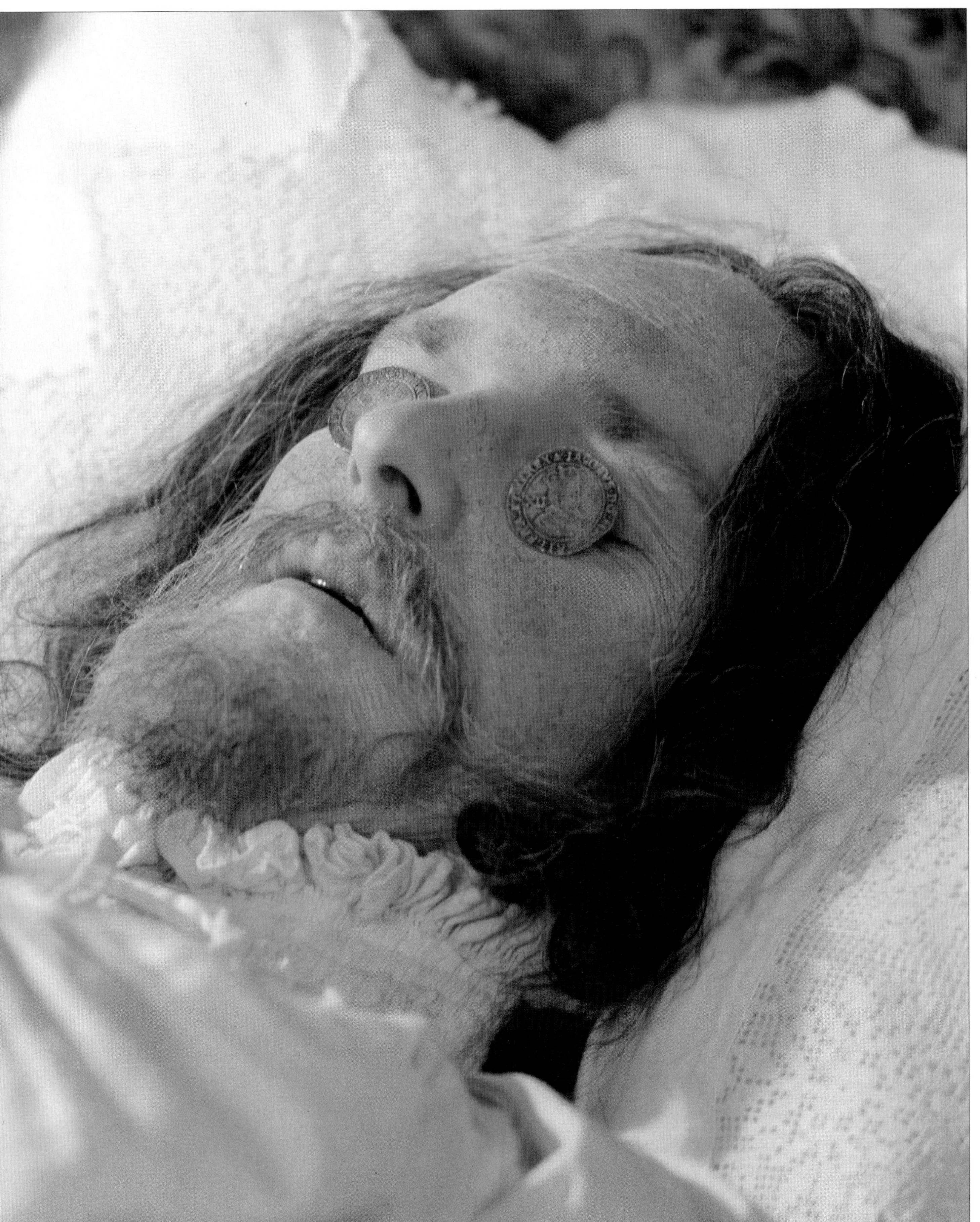

EPILOGUE: AFTER 1616

When Shakespeare died in 1616 his acting company was the most famous and the most successful in the country. They had the King himself as their patron, they had the unique advantage of using two playhouses, one open-air for the summer and a roofed one for the winter, and in their repertoire they had all the plays by England's most popular playwright. They knew that those plays had secured them the status they now enjoyed and the decision to publish all of them as a memorial to Shakespeare was a mixture of pride in their fellow's work and commercial self-interest. They knew that there was some risk of having their plays "borrowed" by other companies, but their high status would ensure their own right to perform the plays would not be challenged. In fact in later years, after the collection had appeared in print, they twice got the Master of the Revels to stop another company from performing them.

The First Folio of 1623 included thirty six plays. More than half of these had not previously been published. As none of his manuscripts of the texts have survived, with the possible exception of the three pages of *Sir Thomas More*, the value of their monument is immeasurable. This first folio did not contain the two long poems or the sonnets, all of which had been in print since 1609 and earlier. The company only had rights to the play-scripts, of course, not the poems, but they were evidently only interested in publishing their fellow's famous plays.

***John Heminges** and Henry Condell undertook the task of sorting out the texts owned by the players and never previously published. They also compared the published texts, including the illegal pirate texts, known as bad quartos, with their own playhouse texts and edited them. Modern Shakespearean scholars reckon that it is the work of a lifetime for one individual to go through all the original versions of the plays to produce a newly edited edition of Shakespeare's works.*

In any case, the players had their hands full just preparing the plays for the press. There was much more to issuing the plays than handing the scripts over to a printer. The deal to publish the First Folio must have taken most of the seven years between Shakespeare's death in 1616 and its eventual appearance in 1623 to set up. Eighteen of the plays were already in print, and the publishers of all these single-play quartos or their successors had the copyright, so only they were in a position to re-issue them. A consortium had to be set up, with the holders of the rights to the already-published plays joining together with new printers to reprint the eighteen in folio size, and add to them the other nineteen or more manuscripts which the King's Men held. This consortium was not ready to start printing until 1622.

There was also the question of the condition of the texts. Some quartos were thoroughly inadequate copies, as the players knew from comparison with the lines they had in their own memories from performance, and the manuscript prompt-books they kept in the playhouse. Some "bad" quartos had already been replaced by more authoritative texts, for instance when the second quarto of *Hamlet* had been issued in 1604 to replace the "bad" first quarto of 1603. But even the 1604 quarto of the play differed in many details from the company's prompt book as it stood in 1622. An Act to restrain the use of oaths on stage had been passed in 1606, so that whereas early play-texts used words like "God" or "the Gods", the later versions had replaced them with "heavens" or some other softer term. The playhouse prompt-books recorded every change made to the text since its first performances. So somebody had to read and edit the whole lot to make sure the best version of each play was made available to the printers of the Folio.

John Heminges, the company's financial manager, and the slightly younger but equally long-serving Henry Condell, took responsibility for the quality of the texts.

Both had been given gifts in Shakespeare's will. They prepared the scripts for the press with the care and loyalty due to their friend's memory and to their company's performance tradition.

It was not an easy task. They did succeed in securing all but one of the eighteen plays already in print for the Folio, the sole omission being the "bad" quarto of *Pericles*. Even if they had possessed a better text of the play they were apparently unable to secure the copyright. Beside negotiating with the various owners of the rights to the quarto texts, they had to check every play to ensure it was a "good" version. They started the process of handing the copies of the plays that existed only in manuscript to the printers by getting their scribe, Ralph Crane, to copy out the first four plays they prepared for the press, but they soon decided that copying one manuscript into another was an unnecessary expense and might introduce new errors. The printers worked from a clear text where possible, and half of the plays already had printed versions. So after Ralph Crane had copied out *The Tempest, Two Gentlemen of Verona, The Merry Wives of Windsor*, and *Measure for Measure*, the first four comedies in the Folio, the editors resorted to using printed quartos, and for the last fourteen of the unprinted eighteen plays the playhouse scripts themselves. That saved one level of new errors being introduced by the scribe, and speeded the production process.

Printing was a laborious business, each letter being set in place with a composer's stick to make a line, and then set with other lines to make a page. Each page was locked into a 'forme' for printing. Eight pages printed on a single sheet, four on each side, made a quarto when the sheet was folded twice. The pages were printed wet, and hung to dry before being folded. Quartos, the routine format for early plays, were at the lower end of the quality scale. The standard of printing was not very high, and proof correction, if any, went on while sheets were going through the pressroom. Plays printed during Shakespeare's lifetime included some which had been assembled by some of the players from memory. It was a kind of theft, and it took the right of ownership from the play company and sold it to a printer. The printer registered the title at Stationers' Hall as a form of copyright, to prevent other printers from reproducing it. Such poor quality quartos are known as "bad" quartos. All printers had to belong to the Stationers' Company, which controlled the trade. Each press had to be licensed, and each book had to be licensed for printing with a fee paid to the Stationers' Company.

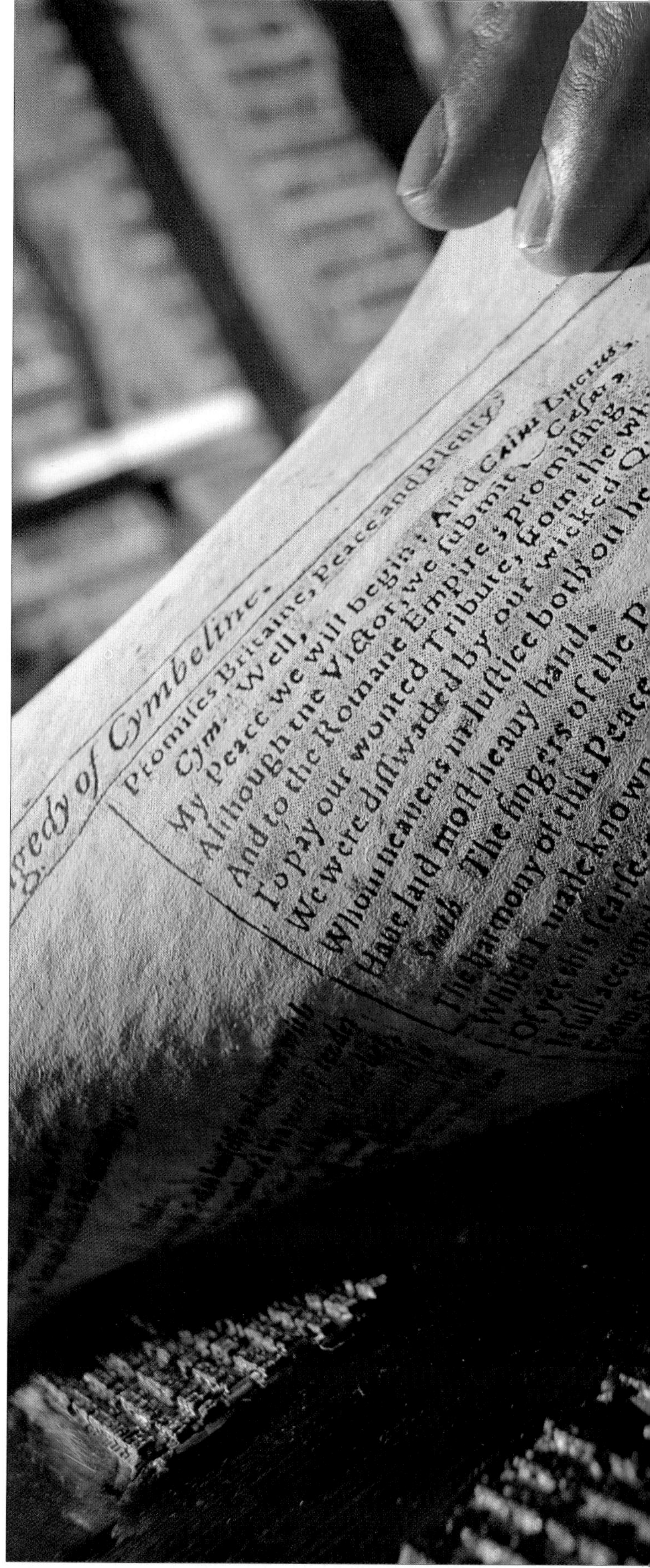

Heminges and Condell checked the quality of most of the quartos against their own prompt-copies. For some plays they chose to give the printers their own manuscripts rather than even the well-printed copies such as the second quarto of *Hamlet*. In others, like *Henry V*, they ignored the "bad" quarto and printed from their playhouse prompt copy, doing some editing of the text on the way. In *Henry V* they inserted act and scene headings, getting it sadly wrong. For other texts they simply checked that the quarto was adequate. In the case of *Richard II* they allowed the printers to set from a quarto text, but in one place where the quarto was inadequate, the deposition scene section of Act IV scene i, they supplied their own better copy from their prompt book. They also put the jumble of plays into a special order, grouping them into comedies, tragedies and histories, although not without some trouble. They had trouble working out whether *Cymbeline* should really belong among the comedies, tragedies, or English histories, since

***Printing** was a laborious task. Production would have begun several years before the whole first folio of thirty six plays was complete. The printers, as well as Heminges and Condell, probably both invested in this memorial to Shakespeare in the hope that it would be a financial success.*

it was a tragicomedy set in ancient Britain, and they had similar difficulty fitting in *Troilus and Cressida.*

All this took several years. The publishing consortium was in place by 1622. Its leader was a publisher called Jaggard, who showed in 1619 that he knew the commercial value of the Shakespeare texts by re-issuing several quartos, illegally using the old title pages and dates to pretend they were the original first editions. The other printers and publishers had more respectable claims to an interest in the Shakespeare plays.

The First Folio sold in 1623 for £1. Any one of the two hundred and fifty copies surviving today would be worth nearly a million pounds. That is an exceptionally large number of copies, compared with the few copies of the single-play quartos, some of which only survive in a single copy, and some not at all. It was a treasured possession for its first owners. It was prefaced by an epistle written by Heminges and Condell. Richard Burbage, the third fellow-player named in the will, had died in 1619. The Folio was also prefaced by a series of poems dedicated to Shakespeare, including the famous epitaph by his friend and rival Ben Jonson. Jonson's judicious and generous assessment said, appropriately enough for the belated publication of his work in a large and impressive book, that he was "not of an age, but for all time".

Having spent £1 on the Folio, buyers were expected to fit their own bindings or covers, usually with their own names and insignia on them. It was a huge price at the time, and only Ben Jonson ever secured the same eminence in having his dramatic works assembled as one book before 1750. As it was, Ben Jonson's Folio had been heavily criticised for its presumption that plays were serious enough to be called "works". Nobody criticised the Shakespeare Folio. Reading printed books of plays had now become respectable.

King Charles I, who had succeeded his father King James I in 1625, was an avid reader of plays and a supporter of play going against the strong disapproval of the mayors of London and the other major cities. The puritan William Prynne who published a book condemning play going in 1633 had his ears cropped, his money confiscated and was put in the Tower for life.

The first Folio soon sold out, and another Folio was issued only nine years later. Two more appeared in the later years of the century. Each contained additional material, some extra poems, copies of the Sonnets, and extra plays, including not only *Pericles* but several other plays which had not been written by Shakespeare at all. These plays are now known as the "Shakespeare apocrypha". They were printed at different times with his name on their title pages to make a better sale.

King Charles I continued his father's tradition by becoming patron of the King's Men. Partly as a result of this favour play going became more and more closely associated in the public mind with royalty. So, when the parliament, dominated by puritans, began to oppose Charles openly after 1640, play going was an early victim. All playhouses were closed by order of parliament at the outset of the English Civil War in October 1642. The Globe was pulled down in 1644. King Charles was beheaded by the revolutionaries in 1649.

The eighteen-year closure destroyed most of the original staging traditions. When the theatres re-opened in 1660, with the restoration of the English monarch King Charles II, the new impresarios introduced French staging, with perspective scenery and proscenium-arch stages. Despite these changes in London, Shakespeare's plays remained popular even with new staging and new editing to suit the new theatres. Shakespeare's plays spread rapidly across Europe, with the sole exceptions of the catholic states of Spain and Italy, which had their own great theatre traditions. In those countries Shakespeare arrived a little later. In Germany a version of *Hamlet* was being played by the 1620s.

In England Shakespeare's reputation was great in his own time and grew rapidly thereafter. The poet laureate to the restored King Charles II, John Dryden, rated Shakespeare as the best of the dramatists in English. By the early eighteenth century new editions of his plays were appearing every decade or so. By the mid-century he had become the image of English greatness, the "Genius of the Nation". This drew attention to his Stratford origins, because Warwickshire was thought to be more "typically English" than the south London suburb of Southwark where the Globe had stood. Scholars began to dig into the Stratford records, chased anecdotes, and started many of the current legends. David Garrick ran an anniversary festival at Stratford in 1769. In the nine-

King Charles I *was patron to the King's Men after Shakespeare's death. As England progressed towards revolution and civil war, the puritan majority closed down playhouses throughout the country and the king was unable to protect his own Men.*

SOIT QUI MAL Y PENSE

teenth century the plays became a stock feature of classroom teaching, and were quoted equally readily by different people on different occasions either as the epitome of national pride, as a model for aristocratic royalism, or as the voice of populist earthiness. There were enough memorable quotations for everyone and everyone made their own version of Shakespeare to suit themselves.

In the twentieth century Shakespeare has become a cultural icon. Seen by some as the epitome of old England, the national poet, his works have been re-staged and rewritten in many different ways. The black Caribbean poet Aimé Césaire wrote a version of *The Tempest*, called *Une Tempete*, making Caliban the key figure as the victim of coloniser Prospero. The same play supplied the plot for the space-age rock musical *Return to the Forbidden Planet*, where every word is a Shakespeare quotation, including the immortal line, "Oh Prospero, Prospero, wherefore art thou Prospero?" Shakespeare today is equally in the possession of educators, theatre producers, and creators the world over. His original words are so strong that they survive transformation.

Modern theatres are as different from the Globe as modern productions are from the original performances. There is a radical contrast for playgoers between standing in the Globe's yard in the rain to watch *Hamlet* standing on stage soliloquizing with a thousand spectators fully visible behind him, and a modern audience in armchairs hidden in the dark watching Hamlet talking to himself lit only by a spotlight. Since Shakespeare originally conceived his plays for the stage and not to be read, the losses we suffer from getting access to his work only on the page or in modernised stage versions are enormous.

***The Swan theatre**, Stratford was built in 1986 within the remains of a previous theatre which had been destroyed in 1879. The modern stage was constructed to represent,as closely as possible, an Elizabethan playhouse.*

Shakespeare's Plays

The following plays are listed in alphabetical order – to see them in chronological order turn to page 182

All's Well that Ends Well

All's Well that Ends Well was written in the first years of the new century, between 1602 and 1604, for the Globe. It was not printed until the First Folio in 1623. It is one of the so-called "problem plays", a comedy written closest in time and form to *Measure for Measure*, with a similar kind of title taken from a well-known proverb. It is a romantic story which in some ways appears to set up a "problem" by questioning the proverbial wisdom of its title. The heroine, Helena, is a girl from a middle-class family, the daughter of a learned doctor. She loves Bertram, the upper-class son of the house where she is living. He does not love her, thinking she is beneath him socially. When with the aid of her father's skill in medicine she cures the sick king, he grants her what she wishes, which of course is Bertram as her husband. But Bertram swears he will not live in marriage with her until she is pregnant by him, and promptly runs off to the Italian wars. There Bertram's gullibility is shown by his friendship with the boastful Parolles, whose hollowness is exposed by the other soldiers. Helena follows Bertram to Italy and gets him to make her pregnant by a version of the "bed trick", also used for the plot of *Measure for Measure*. Nineteenth-century lovers of Shakespeare disapproved of the bed trick device, where one girl persuades another to take her place in the lover's bed. In this play, Bertram is wooing an Italian girl, Diana, so Helena takes her place. In the finale, when Helena's trick is revealed to Bertram, he declares that if she is truly pregnant by him he will keep his promise to love her in marriage. Helena gets her lover, but whether Bertram is worthy of her, and whether he can be expected to let the marriage "end well" is what the audience is left to decide at the close.

Antony and Cleopatra

This is a long-postponed tragic sequel to *Julius Caesar*, written in 1607 or 1608, for the Globe. It was not printed until the First Folio of 1623. It was possibly designed to be Shakespeare's last Roman play and shows the conflict in Antony between Roman politics and Egyptian love. In *Julius Caesar* written in 1599 Antony was revealed as a clever politician ruled by his "affections", his feelings, in contrast to the "reason" which rules his rival Brutus. In the earlier play he proves brilliantly capable of swinging crowds to his side by his manipulation of their emotions. In the later play, his great feelings have made him fall captive to Queen Cleopatra in Egypt. He has a wife in Rome, but he stays in Egypt with Cleopatra. His wife dies, and to cement his political alliances in Rome he marries the sister of his former ally Octavian Caesar. But he cannot keep away from Egypt because of his love for Cleopatra. Antony is defeated in war by Octavian Caesar, who thus becomes at the end of the play the first Roman emperor. So Venus, in the wonderfully attractive person of Cleopatra, conquers Mars, the mighty Roman general Antony. Once the greatest soldier in the Roman world, Antony botches even his suicide in Act IV, when he turns his sword on himself. Cleopatra, always a lover of life, in the end outdoes him in death, triumphantly joining him in her regal suicide in Act V.

As You Like It

THE TITLE OF THE PLAY indicates the kind of light romantic comedy it offers, along with *Much Ado About Nothing* and *Twelfth Night*, which has the subtitle *"What You Will"*. Written in 1599 with several references designed to celebrate the new Globe, it is set in a pastoral "forest of Arden" which is contrasted, sometimes ironically, with the harsher world of the court. The hero, Orlando, has an evil elder brother in the court world, from whom he escapes by fleeing into the forest. There he joins the Duke, rightful ruler of the country, whose place has been usurped by his own brother, and who has fled with his court to live as outlaws in the forest. The outlaws live a life of Arcadian peace. The exiled court includes a handsome singer and melancholy Jaques, who speaks the famous "All the world's a stage" speech, elaborating on the motto of the new Globe theatre. The hero's beloved Rosalind, who is the daughter of the deposed ruler, fell for Orlando when he won a wrestling match at the beginning of the play. The match had been planned by his elder brother as an opportunity to kill Orlando, which is why after winning he flees into the forest. When Rosalind is banished by her uncle the usurping duke she flees into the forest too, along with her best friend the wicked duke's daughter. The court jester Touchstone goes with them. To help them survive in the forest, Rosalind disguises herself as a boy. Touchstone turns himself from a court jester into a country clown, and woos a country wench. When in the forest Rosalind meets Orlando, who is busy declaring his love for her by pinning verses on trees, and who fails to recognise her in her disguise as a boy, she promises to teach him how to woo by making him pretend that she is his beloved. He thus has to put on an act, pretending to woo the boy pretending to be the girl he loves, and who really is his beloved. Thus Rosalind, played originally by a boy player, plays a girl playing a boy playing a girl. The finale unites all the lovers with their proper loves. Orlando's elder brother, banished to the forest too by the wicked duke, meets Rosalind's friend Celia and falls in love with her. Even the wicked duke and his brother whose dukedom he usurped, are won over. Appropriately, after all her actorly disguises and her clever plots to unite the various pairs of lovers, Rosalind speaks the Epilogue.

Cardenio

THIS IS THE ONLY PLAY known to be Shakespeare's that has been totally lost. It was among a list of the King's Men's plays performed at court in 1613. An eighteenth-century editor of the plays, Bishop Warburton, claimed to have owned a manuscript of the play, but reported that his cook Betsy had used it to light his fire.

The Comedy of Errors

This comedy is one of Shakespeare's earliest plays, possibly written before 1590. This delightful play, full of word games, was developed from a comedy by the Roman dramatist, Plautus. Its plot depends on two pairs of identical twins. The twins are separated from one another and their parents by pirates while at sea. One from each set of twins is raised in Syracuse and the other in Ephesus, two cities which were enemies. In each city one twin becomes servant to the other. Landed in Syracuse, the Ephesian twins are involved in a series of confusions as they are mistaken for their Syracusan counterparts. One Syracuse twin is married, but is not on good terms with his wife, so when the Syracusan wife mistakes the identical Ephesian twin for her husband a lot of trouble follows.

Conveniently, she has a sister, and the Syracusan twin promptly falls in love with her. This seems to the sister to be a dreadful disloyalty in a man she loves but thinks is her brother-in-law. The resulting confusions set up a series of knockabout encounters, gloriously ended when the twins come face to face. In the end everyone is reconciled, and even the long-separated parents of the main twins are reunited. The play was commissioned for a performance before the law students of Gray's Inn to boost their Christmas revels in 1594 and proved popular amongst the learned for its rewriting of Plautus. It was not published until the First Folio appeared in 1623.

Coriolanus

Coriolanus was written at about the same time as *Antony and Cleopatra*, in 1608. It is Shakespeare's most contentious, most delicately balanced, and most rewarding political play. It is a tragedy set in the earliest days of the Roman republic, when Rome is only one city amongst several warring with one another on the plains of Latium. The food riot which opens the play echoes the rioting in the English countryside, including Warwickshire, of that year. Coriolanus is the patrician warrior who checks the rioters, and calls them to help him conquer Corioli and save Rome from its threatening neighbours. He defeats the Volscians of Corioli almost single-handed, and, covered in his enemies' blood, is honoured for his valour with the victor's garland and the name of the city he has conquered. His

only acknowledgement of the honour is to say "I will go wash". The kudos of victory makes the Senators, his fellow patricians, put Coriolanus up for election as consul, but he will not submit himself to the new democratic processes of electing Rome's rulers. The patricians of Rome see themselves as owners of the city and the grain which the plebeians want as food. The plebeians, the ordinary people, see Rome as themselves, starved by the rich patricians and driven by their leaders, their tribunes, to exert their newly-won democratic rights gained when they expelled the kings of Rome. In some ways it reflects the political conflicts of 1608 in London, where the king was opposed by lawyers in the House of Commons who their enemies were calling sarcastically 'the tribunes of the people'. Coriolanus refuses to flatter the mob, and his arrogance enrages them. He is banished, losing the name and title that Rome gave him when he won Corioli. He goes to the general he defeated at Corioli and returns leading Rome's enemies to destroy it. None of the pleas of his former friends will stop him. His mother leads his wife and child to him to beg for mercy, and she, the creator of his arrogance, finally persuades him to turn his army away from Rome. He sees far more clearly than she does what she is asking him to do, but accepts her demand. He is subsequently killed by the men of Corioli who he had led against Rome. In this century the play has been performed both as a display of the correctness of right-wing and of left-wing politics. Shakespeare himself, as in so many of his plays, set up a carefully equal balance between the two sides. The play was first published in the First Folio of 1623.

CYMBELINE

CYMBELINE WAS, after *Pericles*, which appeared in 1607, the first of the major plays variously called a 'late comedy', a 'romance', or a tragicomedy. The others were *The Winter's Tale* and *The Tempest*. The editors of the First Folio assigned the latter two to the 'comedy' section, but they had some trouble with *Cymbeline*, dithering between making it a 'comedy' or a 'tragedy'. They might equally well have put it with the third group, the histories, since its subject came from early British history, like *King Lear*. It was written and performed at the Globe in late 1609 or 1610. It is packed with traditional elements from romance, such as a wicked stepmother, a poison that is actually a sleeping potion making the victim appear dead, and a deceitful Italian villain. Its time is ancient Britain at the time of the Roman occupation and the birth of Christ. It mixes two stories. In one of them the king's daughter is married to a man whom the king banishes, and who she sets out to find in the forest. In the other the king's two long-lost sons save their sister from her enemies and re-appear to save the king in battle against the Romans. The banished husband, exiled in Italy, bets with an Italian that his wife will prove immune to any man's seductions. The Italian visits her in Britain and, failing in his attempts to woo her, hides in a chest in her bedchamber and steals her ring while she sleeps. He uses this evidence to claim the bet against her husband. When the heroine, disguised as a boy and hoping to find her husband, is saved from being attacked by her half-brother in a rescue performed by her true brothers, she takes a sleeping potion which her stepmother gave her and which acts on her like a poison. Her brothers, finding what they think is her dead body, speak the most famous and most beautiful elegy ever written, "Fear no more the heat of the sun", over what they think, wrongly, is her corpse. The final act is a long sequence of comically unlikely revelations and reunions.

HAMLET

HAMLET WAS SHAKESPEARE'S most famous tragedy. It was written for the Globe in 1600 or early 1601. It opens with a flurry of confused excitement on the battlements of Elsinor, a Danish castle, where the nervous guards are alarmed to find the ghost of the dead king walk past them. We then meet the court, and see Prince Hamlet grieving at his father's death while the court celebrates his mother's rapid remarriage to her brother-in-law the new king. In a court full of spies and watchers, Hamlet is taken by the worried soldiers to meet the ghost. The ghost of the dead King, his father, tells Hamlet that he was murdered by his brother, and orders him to take revenge. Hamlet, driven almost to distraction by this addition to his other griefs, hesitates, buying time by pretending to be more mad than he really is. The play takes him through many side-tracks before he finally accomplishes his revenge. He thinks of it as not a secret murder like his uncle's killing of his father but an open duel. He uses a 'play within the play' to tell the king that he knows about the murder and that he will murder the murderer. He distrusts all the courtiers around him, including not only two of his fellow-students brought by the king to spy on him, but his beloved Ophelia. Before he faces his uncle he kills his beloved's father, thinking he might be the new king. Her lover's murder of her father drives Ophelia to madness and suicide. Sent to sea, to be murdered in England, Hamlet escapes, contriving the death of the two student spies and finally of Ophelia's brother, who has returned to Denmark to avenge his own father's death on his murderer Hamlet. Hamlet dies himself in this duel with her brother when poisoned swords are used. His mother, the Queen is killed by another poison intended for him. Only when Hamlet knows he is dying himself does he finally kill the king. The play contains several parallels to Hamlet's own revenge. The different choices of revenge are personified first in Hamlet's opposite Fortinbras, revengeful son of a king murdered by Hamlet's father. Then there is Laertes and his sister Ophelia, whose father Hamlet himself murdered. Each of them is drawn to try one of Hamlet's own options voiced in the famous "to be or not to be" soliloquy, suicide or revenge. The revenge options also appear in the two play-actor stories performed by actors visiting the Danish court. One is a speech about King Priam murdered by revenging Pyrrhus, the other their stage-play of the Gonzago king murdered by his nephew Lucianus. There are further echoes in Hamlet's own murders of the various stand-ins for King Claudius, including the counsellor

Polonius who spies on Hamlet for King Claudius. None of Shakespeare's plays is more packed with echoes and auguries of the play's story, revenge as action, both a fictional enactment and a real enactment. The play first appeared in print in a poor copy of the original text in 1603, and was soon followed by a better, more authorised quarto in 1604-5. The Folio edition of 1623 offers a text taken from the company copy, which is different from either of the early quartos.

HENRY IV PART 1

THIS PLAY WAS PRINTED as a quarto in 1597, and reprinted five times up to the Folio of 1623, making it one of the most popular plays of its time. It was the second play in the second and last of Shakespeare's two English history tetralogies. The first tetralogy, or "Henriad", had begun with the reign of Henry VI, and dealt largely with the Wars of the Roses. The later sequence of four linked plays began earlier in history, with the origins of the Wars in the dynastic crisis that started with the usurpation of Richard II's crown by Henry IV. This second "Henriad" or tetralogy began with *Richard II*, written in 1595. Part 1 of *Henry IV* was written in 1596 and first introduced Falstaff to the stage. It continues the story begun in *Richard II*, with Henry IV's usurpation of the English crown, focussing now on the newly-crowned King Henry's worry over his prodigal son Prince Hal. From the outset of the play Hal is contrasted on one side with the heroic Harry Hotspur, who becomes a leader of the main story, the historic rebellion against Henry IV. Hal is contaminated on the other by the sub-plot's story, his friendship with the riotous and law-breaking Falstaff. The rebellion forms the play's serious plot, and the goings-on in Eastcheap with Falstaff the comic sub-plot. Hal promises to himself at the end of the second scene in the tavern at Eastcheap, and later to his father, that he will achieve honour by overcoming Hotspur and show justice by banishing Falstaff. In this play he achieves only the first of these two aims.

HENRY IV PART 2

THIS PLAY WAS FIRST PRINTED in a quarto in 1599. As a sequel, it continues the story of the rebellion against Henry IV, but the neat structure of the beginning of *Henry*

IV Part 1 is overturned. Instead of an equal balance of Hotspur and Falstaff as tempters on each side of Prince Hal, the focus is now mainly on Falstaff and his riotous life in Eastcheap, London, which he takes with him into Gloucestershire countryside. What in Part 1 was the Eastcheap comic sub-plot becomes the main plot, and the rebellion becomes the minor plot. Falstaff is shown as ageing, and avoiding imprisonment by the Lord Chief Justice only through the protection of Prince Hal. Falstaff only meets Hal three times in this play. When Hal and Poins play a trick on Falstaff and pose as tapsters or tavern serving-men there is an echo of their trickily intimate relationship and their marvellously complex game-playing of the first play. But now that is largely set aside. Much of this play is taken up with Falstaff's cynical exploits in Gloucestershire at Justice Shallow's estate, as he recruits his cannon-fodder for the wars. Falstaff's last meeting with Hal is after Henry IV's death when Hal is returning from his coronation as England's new king, Henry V. At that meeting he does finally banish Falstaff. Even then he teeters on the brink of the old games by telling him "know the grave doth gape / For thee thrice wider than for other men". But he quickly realises his mistake, and recovers by ordering "Reply not to me with a fool-born jest. / Presume not that I am the thing I was." The epilogue promises that Falstaff will return in the next play.

Henry V

Henry V's story is essentially what to most Elizabethans was England's finest hour, the battle of Agincourt in 1415, in which a few thousand English soldiers defeated sixty thousand French. This last play in Shakespeare's second series of plays from English history brings the sequence to an end at a point just before the earlier sequence, the first "Henriad", written ten years before, begins. It starts with scenes in which the newly-crowned King Henry V is persuaded that his ancestral claim to the French crown is just, and decides to invade France to secure it. The French king offers him his daughter's hand in marriage and several dukedoms to buy him off, but he scorns them and goes to war. The Eastcheap villains, minus Falstaff, who dies offstage, go to the war for personal profit, but most of them are killed. After the victory at Agincourt Henry accepts the original French offer, including marriage to the princess, although on stage it is presented as a tremendous victory. Uniquely among Shakespeare's plays, this one makes use of a chorus, a speaker who tells the audience what is to happen in each Act to the heroic Henry and his men. He paints vivid pictures in words about Henry's skill as a leader, and the patriotic courage of the English. He colours the story to the audience, sometimes misleadingly, telling them what they should think and what they should expect. He praises Henry as a hero and describes the events that will follow in terms which the succeeding events often call into question. Written in early 1599, at the end of a wearying decade of English wars against the Spanish in the Netherlands, its superficial heroics are undercut by serious questions about military glory. It appeared in 1600 in a quarto printed from what some of the actors remembered as their speeches. A reasonably correct copy from the author's manuscript of 1599 was printed in the First Folio in 1623.

Henry VI part 1

This is the first play in Shakespeare's first tetralogy from English history, a series of four linked plays covering the fifteenth-century Wars of the Roses. It was written only shortly after the Spanish Armada had been defeated in 1588, while English fears about foreign intrusion on the English crown were at their height. The play starts when Henry V, after fathering a son by his French Queen Catherine, has died. This first 'Henriad' opens with his funeral. His son, the infant Henry VI, cannot control his nobles, whose quarrels bring disasters to the English army fighting in France, in its struggle to maintain Henry's title to the French crown against the forces led by Joan of Arc, who seeks to restore the Dauphin, the French king's heir, who had been deposed by Henry V after Agincourt. Amongst the quarreling English nobles, Henry VI's title to the English crown is seen as doubtful because of his grandfather Henry IV's usurpation of the crown from Richard II. This leads to the growth of a Yorkist claim to the crown against Henry's title through the Lancastrian line. The Wars of the Roses, between the red rose of York and the white rose of Lancaster, are heralded in this play, in a scene invented by Shakespeare, staged in the Temple Garden, where the rival followers pluck differently-coloured roses to show their different allegiances. Unlike the three plays in the sequence which followed it, this play was not printed until the First Folio of 1623.

Henry VI part 2

This is the second play in this "first Henriad" or tetralogy, a group of four linked plays, and was written in 1590 or 1591. It begins the long and bloody Wars of the Roses. These were the most feared kind of war, a civil war of English fighting English. The followers of the Earl of York's battle ferociously with Henry's Lancastrians. The pain of civil war is exemplified in a scene when the grieving Henry is made to confront a son who has killed his own father and a father who has killed his own son in battle. In its politics the play shows the intolerable complexity of the question of dynastic title to rule by the law of succession, inheritance by the eldest son, how doubts about the legitimacy of such titles can undermine royal power, and the consequent struggles between strong nobles under a weak king.

HENRY VI PART 3

THIS NEXT PLAY of the sequence was seen by Robert Greene on the London stage in the summer of 1592, where it made a great hit. In it, the Yorkists defeat Henry's Lancastrians. After a brutal series of battles, Henry, captured and held captive in the Tower of London, is murdered by Richard, younger brother to the Yorkist claimant to the crown, who takes the throne as Edward IV. The play colourfully sets Richard, Duke of Gloucester, in position as the monstrous villain who is to become the central character of the final play in the sequence, *Richard III*. A poor quality copy of the play appeared in 1595, but the full text was published only in the First Folio in 1623.

HENRY VIII

HENRY VIII WAS ONE of the last plays which William Shakespeare helped to write. It was most likely planned by the younger playwright John Fletcher, in collaboration with Shakespeare. Staged at the Globe in July 1613, it is a play full of processions and pageantry, with many formal and ceremonious speeches. It covers the middle period of Henry's reign, with the downfall one after the other of Henry VIII's earlier court advisors, the Duke of Buckingham, Queen Catherine of Aragon, his first wife whom he tries to divorce, and the chief agent of the divorce, Cardinal Wolsey. It shows the rise of Anne Bullen (Boleyn) who becomes Henry's second queen, and Archbishop Thomas Cranmer, who becomes his new advisor. It treats the various downfalls as matters for tragic pathos, but it ends on an upbeat note when Ann becomes pregnant with the future Queen Elizabeth. A spectacular play on stage, with ceremonial trumpet-calls and cannon-fire to herald the formal processions and speeches, its popularity was shown by a rare run of three days in succession at the Globe, a unique distinction. Its fame grew still more when at the third performance some wadding from one of the small "chambers", or cannon, fired from the front of the stage cover, lodged in the gallery's thatch, and started a fire which in not much more than an hour burned the playhouse to its foundations. The play was published as Shakespeare's in the First Folio in 1623.

KING JOHN

KING JOHN IS ANOTHER of the many plays which did not appear in print until the First Folio in 1623. It is a complex play which sets out in compressed form the same dynastic issues that were dealt with more extensively in the two "Henriad" tetralogies. As a play about English political issues, it has teased critics for centuries. The evidence suggests with almost equal plausibility that it may have been composed either in 1590 or in 1595. It could be seen as a political statement relating to the politics of its time, but the politics depend on which date is preferred. In 1590 a Spanish invasion was still a real threat, even after the first Armada had been destroyed, and the play deals with such threats to English sovereignty. In 1595 the main issue was the queen's right to rule, and the question of the English succession. In the absence of any children of the ruler, people wondered who would have the authority to name her successor. In the play King John has no heir, and he is implicated in the killing of the alternative ruler, the boy Arthur, just as Elizabeth herself was in the execution of Mary Queen of Scots, who had been considered a possible heir to Elizabeth. King John submitted his power to the Pope, and few Englishmen welcomed that prospect. To many thoughtful people, John's reign was a worrying example of two serious constitutional and political issues that had become dominant in Elizabeth's time. John's own title was doubtful, like Elizabeth's. The play shows him urging the death of the rival claimant to the throne, Arthur, in a way which could be seen as similar to Elizabeth's consent in 1587 to the execution of her potential rival and heir, the Catholic Mary Queen of Scots. John's submission as king to the Catholic Church in order to secure the Pope's endorsement of his title was also a worry. While John is shown uncertain of his way, and dying unhappily, a basic English patriotism and a contrasting valour is shown by Faulconbridge, who is a bastard son of Richard I (just as, by one way of thinking, Elizabeth was the bastard child of Henry VIII). It is teasing to see how the play can fit the political issues of both 1590 and of 1595, in only slightly different ways. The last words in the play are given to Faulconbridge, as the spirit of patriotism, defying "the four corners of the world in arms" to come against the English, a feeling that prevailed throughout the decade after the Armada.

JULIUS CAESAR

A PLAY ABOUT EVENTS in ancient Rome was a fresh start, but a short-lived one. After closing his series of plays based in English history with *Henry V* in early 1599, Shakespeare turned to write the first of what seems to have been planned as a new series of plays based on the Roman histories studied in schools at the time. It starts with the last days of the Republic, the centuries when Rome became great, at the moment when a crown was first offered by some citizens to Rome's great general Julius Caesar to make him the first Roman emperor. That offer started the return of Rome from the form of government that had made it great to the form standard throughout Europe in Shakespeare's time, monarchy. The idea of crowning Caesar worries Brutus and other Senators because they see it as a threat to their Republican liberties, so they conspire to assassinate him. Kings who have no inherited right to the title to rule, but rely only on their charisma as victorious generals, must be tyrants, not rightful kings. Brutus is a stern philosopher and thinker. After the assassination, though, his faith in "reason" fails to secure the mob's sympathy against Mark Antony's disingenuous appeal to their "affections", his famous "Friends, Romans, countrymen" speech which uses sharp sarcasm and some twisted facts to discredit the conspirators. Brutus and Cassius, the two leading conspirators, are subsequently defeated in war by an alliance between Antony and Octavian Caesar, and commit suicide. Brutus's self-doubt helps his side's defeat. The ruthless fighters and politicans win Rome. The play appeared in print for the first time in the great Folio of 1623.

King Lear

King Lear was written in 1605. It was first printed in a quarto in 1608, and in a different version in the First Folio. It is usually acclaimed as Shakespeare's greatest tragedy. Set in pre-Christian Britain, it opens with King Lear announcing that he will divide his kingdom into three, giving one-third to each of his daughters and their husbands, the Dukes of Cornwall and Albany, in return for a public declaration of their love. He himself will live with his youngest, daughter, Cordelia, to whom he has allocated the richest third. Cordelia refuses to make a public declaration, and in fury he banishes her. The older sisters then banish him. A similar pattern works through the sub-plot where the Earl of Gloucester is tricked by his bastard son into banishing his true son. He is then blinded (on stage) by the older daughter's husband, Cornwall, and sent into the storm where he joins Lear, who has been driven mad by the "storm in nature". Cordelia helps to rescue her father, as Gloucester's good son rescues him. In the finale, although Gloucester's good son defeats the evil son, and Lear's two evil daughters kill each other, Cordelia is also murdered. This final monstrosity was Shakespeare's calculated alteration from the source-play, where Cordelia and Lear live happily ever after. In Shakespeare's play it leaves the ending relentlessly bleak. In what may be two different versions of the ending, one written in 1605 and a revision prepared in 1611, the last words are given either to the surviving 'good' husband of Lear's elder daughter, Albany, who shows his incomprehension by trying to divide the kingdom again as Lear did at the opening, or, a little more hopefully, into the mouth of the good Gloucester son. The play was staged at court on Boxing Day 1606, in the presence of King James I. James's older son, Henry, Prince of Wales, was also the Duke of Cornwall, like the modern Prince of Wales. His younger brother Charles, later to become King Charles I, was the Duke of Albany. What the father of the young princes made of this story of a kingdom with a king whose sons-in-law had such familiar names, and the subsequent division of his kingdom, is not recorded. But in 1605 the English Parliament was at odds with King James, who wanted to unite his two kingdoms, England and Scotland. Parliament won this fight, and the union of the two kingdoms was not enacted for another century. By 1611 James's defeat was history. The

play may have been revised then to allow it to be shown at court once more without the pain of reminding James of his earlier hopes. The 1605 text begins with a reference to "the division of the kingdoms". In the 1611 text it has become "the division of the kingdom".

Love's Labours Lost

The play text was first printed in 1599. It is an early comedy, written before 1594. One of Shakespeare's most linguistically elaborate plays, it offers a sophisticated game of elaborate word-play. It opens at the court of King "Ferdinand" of Navarre, named like Lord Strange, the patron of an early acting company which possibly employed Shakespeare as an actor and playwright. King Ferdinand decides to set up a strict academy with his courtiers, where they will study books and never speak to any women. Only one of the four expresses any horror at this unreasonable decision, but it is in any case immediately set aside by a visit from a foreign Princess and her ladies, who have to be received formally at the court of Navarre. The four men immediately fall in love with the four women, and the plot twists around neatly to make fools of their unrealistic attempt to seclude themselves from women. It includes several colourful minor characters who offer a variety of different comic targets, and its climax is a send-up of the locals and their attempt to stage a 'show' of the Nine Worthies. Then, in an unexpected finale, news comes of the death of the Princess's father. The ladies set each of the four men a suitable punishment to endure for a year and a day, after which they agree to receive their love-suits again. Besides its extraordinarily ingenious games of word-play and covert allusions, *Love's Labours Lost* stands today as Shakespeare's most satirical comedy. It mocks and punishes the pretensions and self-deceits of everyone except the four ladies.

Macbeth

Macbeth was written in 1606, and set in Scotland. It deals with King James I of England's Scottish ancestors and some of his concerns with witchcraft. It is dominated by three witches who appear to Macbeth and prophesy that he will become Thane of Cawdor and then king. The king, in reward for Macbeth's service in battle, makes him Thane of Cawdor, and he is then tempted to make sure of the next step in the prophecy. In Act II his wife eggs him on, and they kill the king when he stays at their castle. Macbeth takes the crown, and the king's heirs flee to England. Acts III-V show the succession of murders that follow the murder of the king, in a long descent from Macbeth's uncomfortable eminence. He returns to the witches, who say he will not die from any man born of woman, nor until Birnam Wood comes to Dunsinane. At the end the enemy army carries branches from Birnam as they attack Macbeth at Dunsinane, and Macbeth has to confront the man whose family he has killed, Macduff, who tells him he was not born normally but "untimely ripped" from his mother's womb. The play is packed with vivid images that stimulate such basic human fears as blood, dark night, sleeplessness and nightmares. The story is imaged as a headlong horse race, on the night mare. Macbeth sees himself as trapped in a fatal gallop which leads him relentlessly along the path predicted by the witches. In the finale their words to him prove his capacity to deceive himself. The play first appeared in the Folio of 1623.

Measure for Measure

The play takes its title from the "Sermon on the Mount" of the Book of Matthew in the Bible, and indicates that it is a comedy about justice. Written at about the time King James came to the throne, in March 1603, it opens with two characters, both

determined to re-impose the laws to curb sexuality. The Duke of Vienna has allowed the laws about sexual "liberty" to be relaxed for the last fourteen years. Now he proposes to renew them, and withdraws himself so that a deputy can impose them in his place. At the same time a lady, Isabella, proposes to join the nuns of St. Clare, an order famous for its rigour and its prohibition on its nuns speaking to men. But Isabella's brother is the first man to be caught for illicit sex, and is sentenced to be executed. Isabella has to plead for his life with the Duke's appointed deputy. The deputy is a man set in his new post so that he can be tested by how he uses his position of judge. His sexual feeling is aroused by Isabella, and he tries to seduce her. In the resulting complications all the leading characters, ranging from the idle gallant who has had a child by a prostitute at one extreme, to the Duke and Isabella at the other, are paired off in marriage. The play quietly demonstrates that not even the Duke, the chief judge, is immune to what he has to be judge over. The play's title signals that "measure for measure", just punishment, has to be tempered by mercy, a view strengthened by another familiar biblical saying, "judge not lest ye be judged". This play was another of those first published in the Folio of 1623.

The Merchant of Venice

The text shot into print in a quarto in 1597, not very long after its first appearance on stage. It is a romantic comedy with a hard edge to it. Written soon after the Lord Chamberlain had licensed only the two companies to perform in London, in 1595, it reflects the repertory of the only other company in London, the Lord Admiral's Men playing at the Rose. That company had Marlowe's *Jew of Malta* as one of the favourites in its collection of plays. In 1595 they acquired another, possibly a sequel, called *The Jew of Venice*. Shakespeare's *Merchant of Venice* offered a stage-Jew intriguingly different from the one in the opposite repertory. Its staging in 1595 came a year after London had witnessed the execution of a Portuguese Jew called Lopez, Queen Elizabeth's physician, who was accused (wrongly, as Elizabeth herself believed), of conspiring to poison the queen. Marlowe's play, *The Jew of Malta*, was re-staged at the Rose in 1594, at the time when Lopez was on trial. In Shakespeare's story, the spendthrift Venetian Bassanio tries to make his fortune by winning the rich lady Portia. Portia's father, as a condition of his will, allowed his daughter to marry only the man who chooses the right one from three caskets. Bassanio borrows money from a merchant friend to enter the contest, and the friend has to borrow cash in his turn from Shylock, a Jew who hates the Christian merchant. Shylock offers the money for Bassanio at the risk of the merchant forfeiting a pound of his flesh if he cannot meet the bond. Although Bassanio wins Portia, his friend cannot repay the loan to Shylock in time, and Shylock insists on his pound of flesh. Portia disguises herself as a young lawyer and wins the case by pointing out that spilling any Venetian blood in the process of taking the pound of flesh would make Shylock liable to forfeit all his goods. He is also at risk for threatening to take the life of a Venetian. In order to get off this danger, Shylock is forced to cede half of his wealth to his daughter, who has fled to marry a Christian. Shylock is also forced to turn Christian himself. The financial bonds of Venice are contrasted with the love-bonds at Portia's Belmont. Although the young prodigal Bassanio and the Christian community of Venice win everything, and Shylock loses all he valued, the resolution is not so clear-cut as it appears on the surface. Shakespeare's portrait of a Jew in a Christian community makes much less obvious use of his Jew to expose the hypocrisy of Christian values than Marlowe's play does, but it challenges the more comfortable assumptions of his time no less deeply.

The Merry Wives of Windsor

This is the only comedy that Shakespeare set in his own time and his own country. For all the London scenes of the history plays with Falstaff, he usually chose to set his comedies in a foreign land. The use of local settings was still very new in the plays of this time, and holding up a mirror to the nature of London was evidently not to Shakespeare's taste. Windsor was twenty miles upriver, and its citizens were unlikely to cause much trouble about their portrayal on stage. The play was written either in 1597 or 1599. The 1597 date is attractive because it means the playwright might have chosen Windsor to celebrate the company's new patron, Sir George Carey, who was due to be installed in April of that year as a Knight of the Garter. The Garter ceremony normally took place in St. George's Chapel in

Windsor Palace, and the play might have been composed to mark the festive occasion. In the event the 1597 installation was held in London. The play is an ebullient piece of work, full of eccentric characters and comic knockabout. It may have served to fulfill the promise that Falstaff would not disappear from the stage after being banished at the end of *Henry IV* part 2. It shows an impoverished Falstaff wooing two citizen wives in Windsor. They detect his scheme, and make a fool of him as well as of the jealous husband of one of the wives. Several operas have been made from its story. The play appeared first in a "memorial" version, written down largely from memory, in 1602. A better text appeared in the First Folio.

A Midsummer Night's Dream

This 'Dream' has become one of Shakespeare's most-loved comedies. It was written in 1596, and makes fun of everything from love at first sight to realistic staging. Theories that it was written for a wedding celebration have led to conjectures about more than thirteen different social occasions for which it might have been composed, in the 1590s. The play refers to a "fair vestal throned by the west", which was once thought to have been a polite acknowledgement of the

Queen's presence in the audience. None of the 'wedding celebration' theories fits very well, though, and in any case Shakespeare always wrote his plays as multi-purpose entertainments. The play's story runs through the prelude to a marriage. Set in Athens on the eve of Duke Theseus's wedding to Queen Hippolita, a young girl is told she must accept the man that her father chooses for her husband, not her lover, or else become a nun. These two lovers flee into the forest pursued by the girl's approved lover and her girl rival who loves him. There the fairy king bewitches the men with a potion which forces them to love whoever they first see on awaking, which, after some wonderful confusions when his servant Puck gets his orders wrong, resolves the problem. He does the same to his Queen, from whom he has been alienated. The final Act returns from the night and dream time of the forest to the court, and gives us a play prepared by the "mechanicals", the working men, of daytime Athens to celebrate Theseus's wedding. The play within the play, a literal-minded staging of a classical love story, sends up the kind of concern for stage realism that might try to challenge such improbable and unreal plot devices as magic potions. The play was first printed in a quarto in 1600.

MUCH ADO ABOUT NOTHING

THIS IS A ROMANTIC COMEDY about a love-relationship not dissimilar to the one in *The Taming of the Shrew*, and perhaps is a deliberate rewrite of the earlier play. It certainly exploits the same games of verbal punning and backchat between two reluctant lovers. The older play uses two people forced into marriage who gradually come to value each other, while *Much Ado*'s basic plot is more orthodox, about two strong personalities who see each other as combatants rather than partners. It is sometimes thought to be the play which Francis Meres, a young university scholar, called 'Love's Labours Won' in 1598.It was the first of several comedies starting with *A Midsummer Night's Dream* in 1596 which Shakespeare wrote for a particular pair of boy actors. Two boys played the leading girls' parts in *A Midsummer Night's Dream, Much Ado About Nothing*, and *As You Like It*. The taller boy was dark in hair colour and the other boy small and fair. *Much Ado*'s leading lovers are Benedict and Beatrice, the tall dark boy playing Beatrice. The lovers spar verbally with one another from the outset. Benedict openly scorns the idea of becoming a "married man" to his friends, and Beatrice scorns all men who cannot match her wit. Each is then tricked by their friends into believing that the other secretly loves them. The test of this love comes when Beatrice's friend Hero, betrothed to Benedict's friend Claudio, is spurned at the altar because Claudio has been told that she is unchaste. Beatrice tells Benedict that he must kill Claudio for this insult. Benedict is slowly made to agree to challenge him to a duel. But the local watch, led by the clown Dogberry, originally played by Will Kemp, discover the plot to defame Hero, and tell her father. He tells Claudio and the duke his master, whose brother had told him the lie about Hero, that she has died, and the penitent Claudio agrees to marry whoever her father provides in Hero's place. The living Hero is unveiled to him at the wedding. Benedict then also accepts the status of the married man he had scorned at the beginning. The play first appeared in a quarto in 1599.

OTHELLO

OTHELLO WAS WRITTEN NEXT after *Hamlet* in the sequence of the great tragedies, in 1602-3. It appeared in quarto nearly twenty years later, in 1622, and a rather different version appeared a year later in the First Folio. It is one of the great tragedies. For his basic plot, Shakespeare took two stage stereotypes and reversed them. One character is the black "moor", traditionally a non-Christian from Morocco, the Barbary or barbarian coast of North Africa, who being non-Christian is a murderous villain, like Aaron the Moor in Shakespeare's early play *Titus Andronicus*. The other stereotype character is a simple and honest soldier. Shakespeare opens the play with the opposites of these stereotypes, a soldierly Moor, Othello, a professional general whose work is to defend Venice against the Turks, and a cunningly murderous soldier, with the Venetian name Iago. The Moor has a black face, while the other is dressed like a plain soldier, but in this play the characters that go with these Elizabethan stereotypes are reversed. At this time Moors were famous as warriors, the many struggles between the Spanish and Portuguese and the Moors of the Barbary coast being witnessed by English mercenary soldiers. The fame of Moorish soldiers was most marked by the battle of Alcazar, in which the Moorish army wiped out the entire Portuguese court and army. Some Moors, captured by English pirates in the Mediterranean, were living in London at the time *Othello* was written. There was a Moorish ambassador at Elizabeth's court, and a Privy Council Order was laid down in 1601 to expel all

Moors from London, though it was never enforced. Queen Elizabeth was reported to be "discontented at the great numbers of Negars and blackamoors which are crept into the realm". A head-count identified 164 of them. Shakespeare's play offering a truly noble Moor was written soon after this edict. In the play, Iago's jealousy makes him exploit innocent Othello's marriage to the Venetian Desdemona against him. Iago makes Othello as jealous as himself, until Othello kills his wife. In the finale Iago kills his own wife in a failed attempt to keep his plots secret. Othello kills himself as a just punishment for his misjudgement of Desdemona. At the end the husband and wife, black and white, lie dead together on their marriage bed.

Pericles

Pericles was the first of the so-called "late plays", or tragi-comedies, a type of play written after several years when Shakespeare had written no comedy at all. It was first staged in 1607, and proved hugely popular in its own time, though Ben Jonson, Shakespeare's friend and fellow-playwright, called it "a mouldy tale". Jonson grumbled about all of the late plays, calling them "Tales, Tempests and such-like drolleries." Unfortunately, *Pericles*, for technical reasons largely connected with copy-ownership, was not included amongst the plays printed in the First Folio, so the only text of the play that has survived is a very poor-quality transcript printed as a quarto in 1608. As the first of Shakespeare's new genre, tragicomedy, it has many elements which recur in the other 'late plays'. It starts with a shipwreck in which Pericles is separated from his wife and daughter. The daughter grows up and survives a number of perils, including a stay in a brothel where her virtue proves to be so powerful an influence that it cures the customers. In the end father, mother and daughter are joyously reunited.

Richard II

Richard II was the first play of Shakespeare's second tetralogy, or "Henriad", a group of four linked plays telling stories of English kings. It was written in 1595, the first full year of operation for Shakespeare's new company. It opens with the story of a dynastic crisis, starting in 1399. This second group of plays about English history went back to the period before the first "Henriad", to the origins of the dynastic issues that brought on the Wars of the Roses. Richard II is shown as a rightful king guilty of acting as a tyrant by breaking his own laws. He has murdered his own uncle, and he robs another uncle, John of Gaunt, of his property at his death. This helps him to lose his crown to Gaunt's son Bolingbroke, the Earl of Lancaster, who returns from exile ostensibly to retrieve what Richard had seized from his father, but who is joined by all the discontented nobles when he lands. Bolingbroke also becomes a tyrant through his act of usurpation, deposing the rightful king Richard. He makes a better king but lacks the clear right to the crown that Richard had. At the end of the play one kind of tyrant has replaced the other. Neither has right on his side. The troubles that follow are recorded in the *Henry IV* plays. It proved a popular play for its political similarity to Queen Elizabeth's situation, being printed in three quartos in 1597-8, and another three before the First Folio.

Richard III

A PLAY THAT WAS as famous in its own time as *Romeo and Juliet*, it was the fourth and last play in the first sequence of Shakespeare's plays based in English history, and is dominated by the sinister figure of Richard himself. The historical Richard III was defeated at the battle of Bosworth by the last of the Lancastrian claimants to the English crown, the Duke of Richmond, who became Henry VII, the first of the Tudor kings, grandfather of Queen Elizabeth. The Tudor historians, including Sir Thomas More, painted Richard as a monstrous figure. In the play he is a misshaped monster, whose physical characteristics include the revealing habit of constantly fiddling with his dagger. At the outset he plots to murder his own brother and the young sons of his brother the king, famous as 'the princes in the Tower', to secure the throne for himself. His success in play-acting as he cons one victim after another, both family and noble supporters, with his pretence of innocent purity, is a sequence of theatrical bravura. Once he has the crown, though, he has to go onto the defensive to protect his crown, and his plots begin to fail. As king he faces Richmond, the last heir in the Lancastrian line to the crown, in a battle at Bosworth preceded by a dream in which he is visited by the ghosts of his victims. In the battle he is finally defeated when the Earl of Derby, whose son he is holding hostage, turns against him. The victorious Richmond then ends the civil war between the royal houses of Lancaster and York by declaring that as the Lancastrian Henry VII he will marry the Yorkist heir Elizabeth, so that their children, the Tudors, will unite the two rival lines of succession. The play appeared in six quartos from 1597, and in a rather different form in the First Folio.

Romeo and Juliet

ROMEO AND JULIET WAS WRITTEN early in Shakespeare's career, possibly before 1594. It became one of the favourite plays in the new Chamberlain's Company repertoire after that time. Shakespeare was a performer in this company of players from its creation in 1594, and *Romeo and Juliet* made his name as much as did his poem *Venus and Adonis*. The play was quoted by law students and gentry as a model of good blank verse. Based on an old narrative poem, it was radical for its time in rating love at first sight as more important in making a good marriage than the authority of parents, and their right to choose husbands for their daughters. It tells of two young lovers in Verona who belong to families which are enemies. In the end the enmity between the two families kills both of the well-meaning lovers, and forces the bereft families to unite in grief. The most famous of the early tragedies, its ferocious story of love, human insensitivity and tragic mistakes made it Shakespeare's most popular play in its own time and ever since. Its evident moral has made it a play frequently adapted into modern settings. A poor quarto published in 1597 was replaced by a better copy in a quarto of 1599.

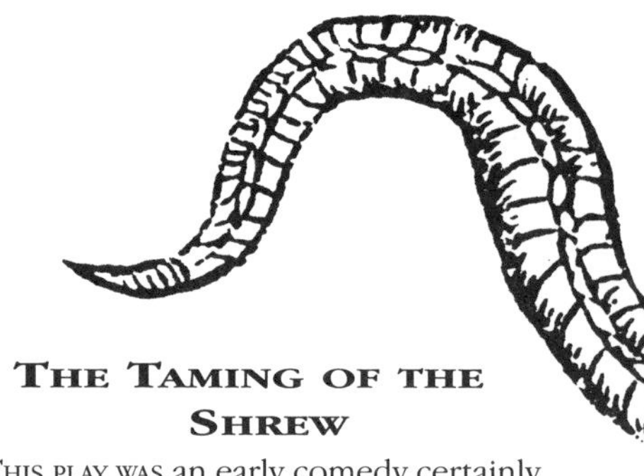

The Taming of the Shrew

THIS PLAY WAS an early comedy certainly written by 1593. It is set in Italy, like most of the popular comedies and prose novels of the time. But it reverses the usual pattern of romantic comedy, by dealing not with the wooing of young lovers but with life after marriage. Katherine is the elder daughter of a rich nobleman. She has the reputation of a sharp tongue and bad temper, whereas her younger sister, who is blonde and charming, is favoured by her father and has lots of suitors. Katherine's bad temper is due more to her father's attitude than to her jealousy of the flock of young men who admire her younger sister and ignore her. But in this society the elder daughter must get married first, so all the younger daughter's suitors, and her father, harried by Kate's shrewishness, welcome Petruchio, who

arrives to make a rich marriage and therefore agrees to take on Katherine sight unseen. The heart of the play shows his process of gradually "taming" her till she starts to share his own eccentric ways. By the end they prove to be true lovers, while Kate's younger sister Bianca, now also married, proves herself to be a shrew.

A quarto printed in 1594 under the name "The Taming of A Shrew" seems to be a rewrite of Shakespeare's original text, which was not published until the 1623 First Folio.

The Tempest

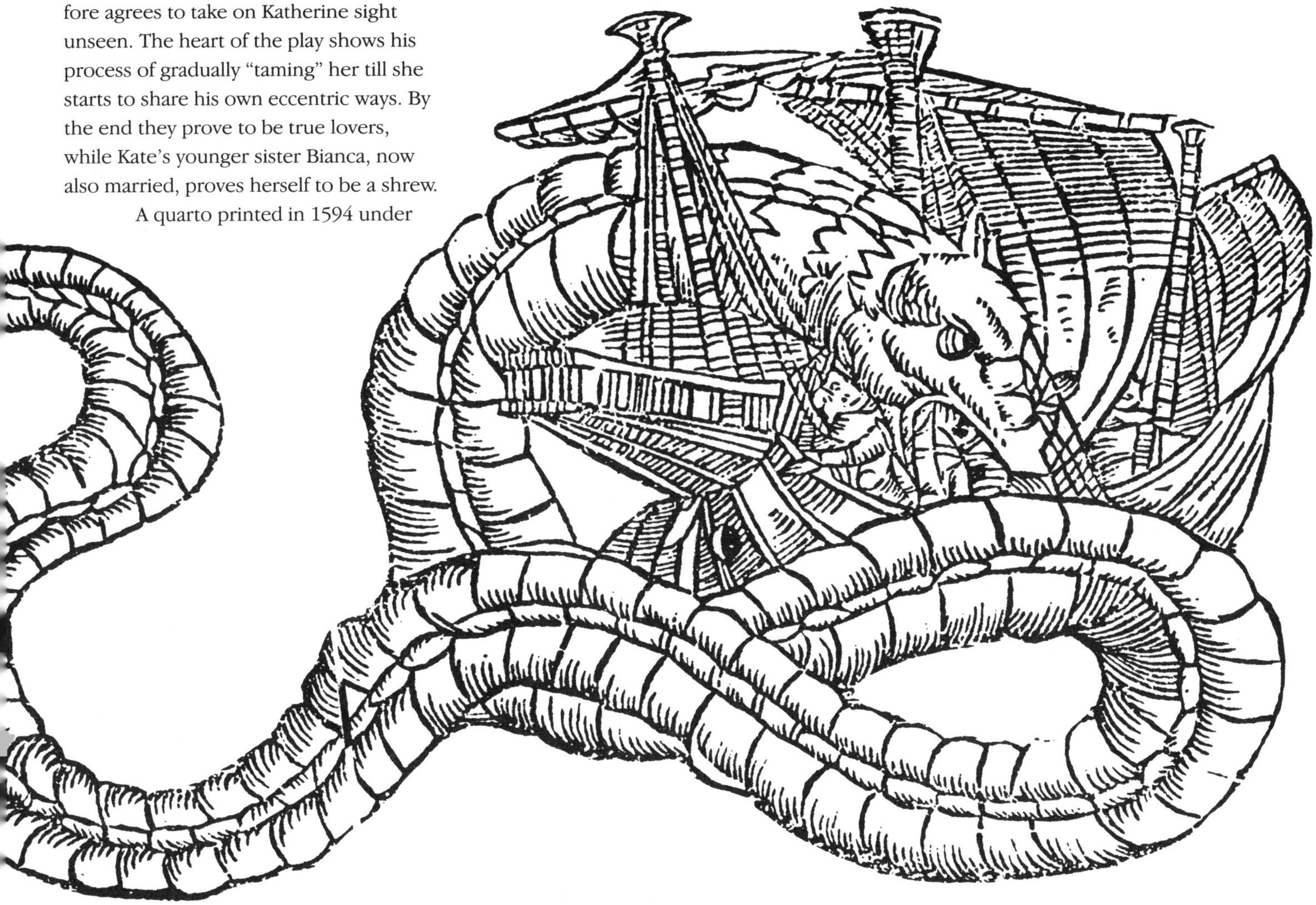

This was possibly the last play Shakespeare wrote unaided. It is set on a desert island, and lasts in real time hardly longer than the actual length of the play itself. Its main character is a magician, a curious coincidence since it was written in 1610, just when Ben Jonson was composing his own play *The Alchemist*, also about a magician, and also for Shakespeare's company. Jonson's alchemist is a fake magician, a con-man, but Shakespeare's is a real master of magic. His magic works like a metaphor for theatrical magic, the art of deceiving a theatre audience into believing they are watching a real tempest at sea. The magician is Prospero, the Duke of Milan, who has been marooned with his daughter on the island, where he has learned the magic that enables him to control the elements. On the island he secures the shipwreck of his enemy the King of Naples together with his son, and Prospero's own usurping brother, who stole the Milan dukedom with the king of Naples's help. Prospero has two servants, the spirit Ariel and the earthy servant Caliban, a witch's child. Prospero's plan is to use the pretended shipwreck to capture his enemies who exiled him, and to get his daughter and the king of Naples's son to fall in love with each other. This neatly reconciles the political enmity between Milan and Naples, and restores the dukedom to Prospero. At the end they all return to Naples except for Ariel, who is freed, and Caliban, whose fate is left unclear. Prospero himself speaks the epilogue, and this together with others of his speeches have led many audiences to interpret his voice as that of Shakespeare saying farewell to his theatrical art. If so, it seems that Shakespeare composed his self-image as a distinctly bad-tempered and absent-minded plotter, dependent on agile youths to do his work for him. *The Tempest* was printed as the first of the comedies, and is therefore at the beginning of the First Folio.

Timon of Athens

As a play, it may never have appeared in public until the First Folio in 1623. It is rarely performed, and was possibly never finished. It dates from the period of Shakespeare's lowest output, 1604 to 1607. Its second half largely consists of a monologue by Timon, self-exiled and hating the world. There is no evidence that it was ever staged in Shakespeare's own time, and it has not been staged often in the subsequent centuries. Almost more a philosophical play than a tragedy, it tells the legend of a rich Athenian, Timon. His ample generosity is exploited by his followers in the first half of the play until halfway through he renounces them all. The second half shows him alone in a deserted landscape, visited only by a few people such as Alcibiades, an exiled Athenian politician. He debates life and materialism with them in some extraordinarily intricate arguments, intense but with little dramatic incident and no radical action in the story. The verse shows Timon ranging through all the arguments for taking a friendly view of mankind, and finding them wanting. It concludes with his total renunciation of life and his death.

Titus Andronicus

Titus Andronicus first appeared in a quarto in 1594. It was possibly Shakespeare's first tragedy, written some time between 1590 and 1593. It uses classical mythology in the setting of ancient Rome to analyse the subjects that all of the later tragedies deal with, but in a more concentrated and far more bloody form. It opens in Rome with a competition for the new emperor. The eldest son claims his right to the empire by primogeniture, inheritance by the eldest son, while the younger son claims his own superior worthiness, which could make him ruler by election. As a third choice, the people propose Titus, the victor in war over Rome's enemies, for their emperor. Titus himself, however, opts for the traditional English model, inheritance by the eldest son. Disaster follows. The emperor's reign becomes evil when he is seduced by one of Titus's captives, Tamora, Queen of the Goths. Helped by Aaron, an evil Moor, her sons rape Titus's daughter Lavinia. To prevent Lavinia revealing who did it they cut off her hands and her tongue. She, however, following the classical precedent of the rape of Philomel, takes a stick and writes their names in the sand. In revenge Titus adapts the Greek legend of Thyestes. He kills the sons and puts their remains into a pie which he serves up to their mother. The play, hailed in its own time for its great verse and its rewriting of the classical models, is by some way the most bloody of all Shakespeare's tragedies.

Troilus and Cressida

Troilus and Cressida is one of the greatest enigmas among Shakespeare's plays. Written at about the time of *Hamlet* and *Twelfth Night*, in 1601 or so, it has sometimes been called a 'problem play', like *Measure for Measure* and *All's Well*, which were written shortly after. It is the only play he wrote that is set in the ancient Greece of Homer's Troy, which makes it the earliest in historical time of any of the plays. *Troilus and Cressida* uses a story celebrated also by Chaucer, Henryson, and other medieval British poets. The editors of the quarto of 1609 who hailed its appearance as a new play, and the editors of the First Folio in 1623, could not decide whether to call it a comedy or a tragedy. They were only the first among a myriad of readers and critics who had trouble working out its genre. It is variously a tragedy, a romantic comedy, and a satire. In fact it has elements of all of these genres, dextrously woven together to make a play designed to challenge any easy pigeonholing. It contains both a "sweet fool", Cressida's Trojan uncle Pandarus, and a "bitter fool", the ranting Greek cynic Thersites. It has the great lovers of the title, a classic story of love betrayed which immortalised the lovers' names and made 'to pander' into a mocking byword for someone who provides sex for others. It has the greatest of Greek heroes Achilles and the greatest Trojan hero Hector, and shows Achilles shamefully contriving the murder of Hector, who for all his wise counsel to the Trojans to stop the war cannot avoid the temptation to indulge himself in personal combat with the Greeks. It has been read as a cynical satire on sexual love, and as a satire on men's lust for war, and is undoubtedly both. Its poetry is so intricately knotted in a series of running metaphors, including time, and sex as food (it has the first known reference to herpes as a sexual disease, presented as the risk of burning your lips if you eat your newly-baked cake while it is too hot). Sex is imaged as a recurrent appetite on which people make themselves sick. All this is set in a study of male and female concepts of honour in the mixture of love and war. It has been called the great study of love as the conqueror of heroes. It has been seen as a play so intense in its complexity that, critics have suggested, it must have been written not for the common playgoer at the Globe but for a special audience, probably a meeting of the law students at one of the Inns of Court. The publisher of the first quarto in 1609 claimed that it had never been "clapper-clawed with the palms of the vulgar". Possibly it had not been revived after its first performances some time before February 1603, when it was first entered for publication in the Stationers' Register.

Twelfth Night

Twelfth Night is the most intricate of Shakespeare's great middle-period comedies. Written just after *Hamlet*, in 1601, it plays the familiar games of the time with boys playing girls who dress as boy pages, with confusions of identity, and the confrontation of puritan rigour with festival. In its own way it could be read as a defence of the Shakespearean comedy of love and the festive element in life against the satirical or 'railing' kind of comedy that Ben Jonson had written for the Chamberlain's Men, plays in which Shakespeare performed. *Twelfth Night* is set in a never-never land called Illyria. It starts with a girl landed on a hostile shore from a shipwreck in which she fears her twin brother has drowned. For protection in a strange country she dresses in his clothes as a boy, and joins the court of Illyria's ruler, Duke Orsino. She becomes

Orsino's page. He is languishing for love of the lady Olivia, who has sworn that because of her brother's recent death she will wear mourning for seven years and not consider love. The girl page falls in love with the Duke, and Olivia falls in love with the girl page thinking she is a young man. The play has elements of all the earlier comedies, with mistakes over the identity of the girl dressed as a boy and her identical twin, who of course is not drowned, and appears in time to fall in love with and promptly marry Olivia. The Duke is outraged at what he thinks is his page's disloyalty, but the girl, not yet having seen her brother, cannot understand what has upset him. All is revealed when the twins meet each other, and the right marriages follow. The play has an elaborate sub-plot, chiefly in the form of a clash between Olivia's festive uncle and her jester Feste on the one side, and her puritanical steward Malvolio on the other. The festive group trick Malvolio into thinking that Olivia loves him, and so to dress outrageously as a would-be lover. He is put in a cell under the stage for what is assumed to be his lunacy before the trick is revealed to him. The play was not printed until the First Folio of 1623.

The Two Gentlemen of Verona

This play was one of the earliest of Shakespeare's romantic comedies. It must have been written soon after 1590. One theory argues that it was written for a company of boy players, although since the last of these stopped playing in 1590 that does not seem very likely. The play concerns two pairs of lovers. The two young men, who are close friends, leave Verona and meet again in Milan. One of them is already betrothed, but in Milan they both fall in love with the same woman, Sylvia. Proteus, the changeable lover who has left his lady in Verona, becomes his friend's rival. His loyal lady Julia dresses as a page to follow him, and after some desperate adventures, including capture by brigands, with Sylvia helping the forlorn Julia, both pairs of lovers are united. The play develops some lively dilemmas for the lovers, and tests love between the sexes against male friendship. At the finale the nobler of the two young men actually tries to renounce Sylvia, offering to give her to his faithless friend. Fortunately he ends up making the wiser choice. In the later years when the play was staged its single most celebrated character usually turned out to be a dog, Crab, who belongs to the clown, and who

is addressed regularly by his owner, though he never has anything to do except walk on stage with his master. The play was not printed until the First Folio of 1623.

The Two Noble Kinsmen

This play text first appeared in print in 1634, ascribed to "the memorable worthies of their time, Mr John Fletcher and Mr William Shakespeare". Written in 1612 or 1613, along with the lost *Cardenio*, it belongs to the new fashion that Shakespeare had been cultivating for the Blackfriars and Globe audiences since 1608, with *Pericles, Cymbeline, The Winter's Tale* and *The Tempest*, and the first of the Beaumont and Fletcher team's tragicomedies, *Philaster* and *A King and No King*. Fletcher also collaborated with Shakespeare in *Cardenio* and *Henry VIII*. *The Two Noble Kinsmen*'s story is based on Chaucer's "Knight's Tale" from *The Canterbury Tales*, a work Shakespeare had borrowed from previously for *A Midsummer Night's Dream*. In essence, it is the story of two gentlemen who love the same woman. As in *Two Gentlemen of Verona*, and unlike *A Midsummer Night's Dream*, they have to choose between love and friendship, and their debate over the choice they should make shows the crucial principles that should control honorable and gentlemanly behaviour. Palamon and Arcite decide on a duel. The winner is to have the lady, while the loser is to be executed. Palamon loses, and is about to be executed when news comes that Arcite has fallen from his horse and is dying. Before he dies, he renounces the lady in his friend's favour. Duke Theseus, the

lady's brother-in-law, closes the play with a speech about how whimsical Dame Fortune is.

The Winter's Tale

This play was a late tragicomedy, written in 1609-1610. It has some connection with *The Tempest*, and also with Ben Jonson, who returned to write for the King's Company with *The Alchemist* in 1609-10. Ben Jonson was a firm believer in the neo-classical rules for drama, and particularly the 'unities' of action, time and place. He had no liking for the "late play" style of tragicomedy with its multiple plots that Shakespeare was now writing along with the younger playwrights Beaumont and Fletcher. It may be that even before they started working together again in 1609 on their two magician comedies, *The Alchemist* and *The Tempest*, Shakespeare had started to poke quiet fun at Jonson's outspoken views about the 'unities'. *The Winter's Tale* ranges through sixteen years in time, marked by the choric figure of Time himself, and through a fantastic geographical range from Sicily to Bohemia. He took his story from an old romance, *Pandosto*, by his old enemy Robert Greene, and reversed the geography, so that instead of starting in the kingdom of Bohemia and then fleeing to shipwreck on the coast of Sicily, the play starts in Sicily and the wreck happens on the sea-coast of Bohemia, an inland country. Jonson certainly noted this anomaly, because he later complained that Shakespeare had given Bohemia a coast where "there was no sea by two hundred miles". Shakespeare was baiting Jonson, and he swallowed the bait. The play starts during a visit by Polixenes, the king of Bohemia, to his friend the ruler of Sicily, Leontes. Leontes is suddenly obsessed by the conviction that his wife Hermione is pregnant from an affair with Polixenes. When Polixenes is told of this and flees, Leontes imprisons Hermione pending a judgement on the truth of his allegation by the Oracle at Delphi. She gives birth, and he orders the baby to be left on a seashore for wild beasts to devour her. The Oracle pronounces Hermione to be faithful just as Leontes hears that his ten-year-old son is dead and that Hermione has died too. That is the tragic half of the play. It ends on the sea-coast of Bohemia with the courtier who maroons the baby being eaten by a bear and the baby being found by shepherds. Sixteen years then pass, with the help of Time, who gives a choric speech, before the comic half begins. A young shepherdess, the baby found by the shepherds, is shown at a pastoral fair with her lover, the disguised son of King Polixenes. Polixenes discovers their love, and they flee to Sicily. There all turns out well. In a revelation scene Hermione's statue comes to life, and the forthright lady Paulina reveals that she has been keeping her safe for the last sixteen years, however improbably, "like an old tale still", until she can be reunited with Leontes. The Oracle said that all would be well once the lost child was found, as she now has been. The children are likewise reconciled and reunited with their parents in the finale. the play was printed originally in the First Folio of 1623.

CHRONOLOGY OF SHAKESPEARE'S PLAYS

Play	Date	Playhouse
	1587	
	1588	
The Two Gentlemen of Verona	1589?	Theatre?
The Comedy of Errors	1589?	Theatre?
King John	1590/1595	Theatre?
Henry VI part 1	1590?	Rose
Titus Andronicus	1591?	Theatre?/Rose
Henry VI part 2	1592	Theatre?
Henry VI part 3	1592-93	Theatre?
The Taming of the Shrew	1593?	Theatre?
Richard III	1593?	Theatre?
Venus and Adonis	1593	printed 1593
The Rape of Lucrece	1594	printed 1594
Love's Labours Lost	1594?	Theatre?
Sonnets	1594-99?	printed 1609
Romeo and Juliet	1594?	Theatre
A Midsummer Night's Dream	1595?	Theatre
Richard II	1595	Theatre
The Merchant of Venice	1596	Theatre
Henry IV part 1	1596	Theatre
The Merry Wives of Windsor	1597	Curtain
Henry IV part 2	1597	Curtain
Much Ado about Nothing	1598	Curtain
Henry V	1599	Curtain/Globe
As You Like It	1599	Globe
Julius Caesar	1599	Globe
Troilus and Cressida	1600?	Globe
Hamlet	1600	Globe
Twelfth Night	1601	Globe
All's Well that Ends Well	1602?	Globe
Othello	1603?	Globe
Measure for Measure	1603	Globe
Timon of Athens	1604?	Globe
King Lear	1605	Globe
Macbeth	1606	Globe
Pericles	1607	Globe
Coriolanus	1608	Globe
Antony and Cleopatra	1608	Globe
Cymbeline	1609	Globe
The Winter's Tale	1609	Globe
The Tempest	1610	Blackfriars/Globe
The Two Noble Kinsmen	1611?	Blackfriars/Globe
Cardenio	1612?	Blackfriars/Globe
Henry VIII	1613	Globe
	1614	
	1616	

	Event
	Mary Queen of Scots executed
	The Earl of Leicester dies ● The Spanish Armada
	Jew of Malta first staged
	Boy companies closed ● first parts of *Faerie Queene* and *Arcadia* published
	Greene's *Orlando Furioso*
	Alleyn opens at the Rose ● Greene dies ● long plague closure begins
	Second Spanish Armada wrecked
	Marlowe dies
	Bad harvests begin ● Formation of Chamberlain's and Admiral's Men
	Drake and Hawkins die ● Swan playhouse opens
	Essex's Cadiz expedition ● Raleigh's *Discovery of Guiana* published
	Blackfriars theatre built ● Hamnet Shakespeare dies
	Theatre playhouse closed
	Third Armada shipwrecked ● Bacon's *Essays*, King James's *Daemonology* published ● Jonson imprisoned for offensive play
	Lord Burghley dies ● Chapman's *Iliad* I - VII published
	Essex fails in Ireland ● Globe opens
	Boy companies reopen
	Fortune opens ● Kemp dances to Norwich
	Essex coup and execution ● Nashe dies
	A third adult company approved
	Queen Elizabeth dies and King James succeeds ● closure of theatres because of plague ● James makes peace with Spain
	James issues *Counterblast to Tobacco* ● Red Bull opens
	Gunpowder Plot ● Jonson works with Inigo Jones on Court masques ● Bacon's *Advancement of Learning*
	Paul's Boys company closes
	Long plague closure
	King's Men acquire Blackfriars
	theatres still closed
	English colonise Ulster ● Bermuda pamphlets written
	'Authorized Version' of Bible issued ● Chapman's *Iliad* completed
	Prince Henry dies
	Burning of the Globe ● Princess Elizabeth marries Elector Palatine
	Globe rebuilt ● Hope opens
	Shakespeare dies ● Cockpit opens

Chronology of the world during Shakespeare's lifetime

Date	England, Scotland and Ireland	Rest of Europe
1564	Shakespeare born	Galileo born Michelangelo dies
1565	Manufacture of pencils begins	La Valette defends Malta successfully against Turks
1566		Beginning of unrest in Netherlands Rebellion and suppression of Christianized Moors in Spain
1567	Mary Queen of Scots forced to abdicate	
1568		
1569		Union of Lublin establishes political unity in Poland Gerard Mercator's map of the world founds modern cartography
1570	Papal Bull excommunicates Elizabeth I	
1571		Battle of Lepanto; Austrians end Turkish sea power in central Mediterranean
1572		Dutch revolt against Spain in war of liberation
1573		Jesuits begin counter reformation in Fulda
1574		Fifth war of religion in France
1575	Queen Elizabeth declines sovereignty of the Netherlands	Second national bankruptcy of Spain Child labour abolished in Hungarian mines
1576		Edict of Beaulieu allows reformed religions in France, except Paris Spaniards sack Antwerp Pacification of Ghent unites all Dutch provinces against Spain
1577	Drake begins voyage around world	Rubens, Dutch painter, born
1578		
1579		Southern Netherlands recognise Philip II of Spain
1580	First commercial treaty between England and Turkey Drake's voyage around world completed	Seventh war of religion in France Philip II conquers Portugal Frans Hals, Dutch painter, born
1581		Northern Netherlands renounces allegiance to Spain
1582		Gregorian calendar introduced to Roman Catholic countries
1583		
1584		Potatoes first imported to Europe
1585		Antwerp sacked by Spaniards
1586	Trial of Mary Queen of Scots	War between the three Henrys of France
1587	Mary Queen of Scots beheaded	

	The Americas	Asia	Rest of the world
	Spaniards destroy Huguenot colony in Florida	Akbar extends Mughal power to Deccan	
		Akbar conquers Chitor	
		Spanish conquer the Phillippines	Portuguese create colony in Angola
	Francis Drake begins attacks on Spanish harbours in America		
	Drake sees the Pacific ocean from Isthmus of Panama	Akbar annexes Gujarat	
		Akbar conquers Bengal	
		Russians cross the Urals	Portuguese power destroyed in N. W. Africa
	Drake proclaims English sovereignty over New Albion (California)	Portuguese trading station in Bengal	
		Russians begin conquest of Siberia Akbar subdues Afghanistan	
		Jesuit mission in China begins	
	Raleigh discovers and annexes Virginia	Phra Narai creates independent Siam	
	Raleigh starts colonising Virginia		
	Raleigh abandons colonisation of Virginia		
	Second English settlement in Virginia fails	Akbar annexes Kashmir	

Date	England, Scotland and Ireland	Rest of Europe
1588		Spanish Armada defeated by English
1589		Henry III of France murdered. Henry of Navarre claims crown
1590		Janssen invents the microscope Alexander of Parma attacks Henry IV of France
1591		English and German troops assist Henry IV
1592		Alexander of Parma dies The remains of Pompeii discovered
1593	London theatres closed by the plague	Henry IV of France becomes a Roman Catholic
1594	Earl of Tyrone revolts in Ireland	The French painter Poussin born
1595	Raleigh's first expedition to Guiana	Henry IV declares war on Spain
1596		England, France and Netherlands ally against Spain Descartes, French philosopher, dies
1597		Spanish naval expeditions against England fail
1598	Tyrone victorious in Ireland	Peace between France and Spain
1599	James VI of Scotland asserts Divine Right of Kings Essex makes treaty with Tyrone	First postal rates fixed in Germany
1600	New rising of Tyrone English East India Company founded	
1601	Essex beheaded	Postal agreement between France and Germany
1602		Persecution of Protestants in Hungary
1603	Queen Elizabeth I dies; James VI of Scotland proclaimed King of England, Scotland, France and Ireland as James I	
1604		Peace between England and Spain
1605	Gunpowder plot discovered	
1606	Guy Fawkes executed	Rembrandt born
1607	Ulster estates confiscated and given to English and Scottish settlers. Tyrone flees to Rome	Monteverdi establishes opera as art form
1608		First mention of forks in Italy
1609		12 years truce between Spain and Netherlands Netherlands ally with England and France Telescope invented
1610		Kepler, founder of modern astronomy, dies
1611		
1612		
1613		Peace between Sweden and Denmark
1614		Civil war in France for 3 months
1615		Second Civil war in France
1616	Shakespeare dies	Cervantes, author of *Don Quixote*, dies

	The Americas	Asia	Rest of the world
		Akbar conquers Orissa	
			Moroccans destroy Songhai kingdom
		Japanese begin to conquer Korea Akbar conquers Sind	Portuguese settle at Mombassa
		Lancaster breaks Portuguese monopoly in India Akbar takes Kandahar	
			Dutch colonise East Indies
		Chinese expel Japanese from Korea	
		Time of Troubles in Russia	
		Akbar begins to subdue Deccan	
		William Adams lands in Japan	Oyo Empire in Africa at height of power
		Akbar annexes Khandesh	
	Champlain's expedition to Canada	Beginnings of Kabuki theatre, Japan	
	French settle in Acadia (Nova Scotia)		
	First permanent English settlement in America (Jamestown)		
	French colonists found Quebec		
		Beginning of Tokugawa Shogunate in Japan	
		First British envoy to Great Mogul	
	Bermudas colonised from Virginia		
		English settlement permitted at Surat, India	
	Virginian colonists prevent French settlements in Maine and Nova Scotia		
		Manchu Tartars invade China	

INDEX

K

L

M

N

O

P

Q

R

S

T

U

V

W

XYZ

Publisher's Acknowledgements

To produce a book like this requires an enormous commitment from the team that create it. In addition to those acknowledged in the front of the book, literally hundreds of people were prepared to turn up in good weather and in bad and at highly unsociable hours to take part in the various recreation scenes that appear in the book. We would like to thank them all, in particular Marcus Barron who became our William Shakespeare.

Finding suitable photographic locations was a complicated task. We had to find buildings which, for one reason or another, had remained essentially unchanged since Shakespeare's time. After much searching we would like to thank the owners, who often at considerable inconvenience to themselves, allowed us to use their fine and historic buildings for photography. We would like to thank Judith and Patrick Phillips of Kentwell Hall, Long Melford, Suffolk; Anna and John Mosseson of Otley Hall, Otley, Ipswich, Suffolk; Sheila and Nicholas Charrington of Layer Marney Tower, Layer Marney, Colchester, Essex; The Town Council at Hadleigh, Suffolk for permission to use the Guild Hall; and the International Shakespeare Globe Centre for permission to photograph Shakespeare's Globe in London. Some of the families who live in these historic homes were suffieniently impressed by this project to join in themselves. Tobias and Natasha Phillips were respectively a page to Queen Elizabeth I and a milk maid and John Mosseson, as Francis Collins, guided Shakespeare's hand over his final will.

With the exception of Shakespeare's Globe in London, all the above houses and buildings are located in that part of England known as East Anglia. For various historical reasons a large part of this area has escaped modern urban development which meant it was ideal for our purposes. A photographic crew descended on the tiny village of Highham in Suffolk and we would like to thank all those who we stayed with for putting up with our long hours. We would particularly like to thank Charles Fenwick and Daphne Dormer, John and Meg Parker, Patrick and Jennie Jackson, Penny and Noel Watkins, Penny Potter and Elizabeth and Caro Gurney. We would also like to thank John and Julian Coulson who were incredibly helpful during our stay.

During the planning stage of the project we received a great deal of help from the late Marion Weir and her daughter Katharine Bowry who kindly read and corrected the manuscript. We would also like to thank Alex and Tessa Scrope for their constant support as well as Arianne Gastambide.

Engravings, maps, paintings and illustrations appear in the book by courtesy of the following sources.

British Library/The Bridgeman Art Library, London
The Governors of Dulwich College
Mary Evans Picture Library
The Fitzwilliam Musueum, University of Cambridge/The Bridgeman Art Library, London
The Guildhall Library, London
Walter Hodges/Oxford University Press
Peter Jackson
Simon McBridge/Royal Shakespeare Company
Philip Mould, Historical Portraits, London/Bridgeman Art Library, London
The National Maritime Museum, Greenwich
Temple Newsam House, Leeds/Bridgeman Art Library, London
The illustrations on pages 162-181 are taken from contemporary illustrated books.